Jagdgeschwader 52

The *EXPERTEN*

OSPREY
PUBLISHING

Jagdgeschwader 52

The *EXPERTEN*

John Weal

Series editor Tony Holmes

Front Cover
Mark Postlethwaite's specially-commissioned cover painting captures to perfection the scene as Leutnant Erich Hartmann claims both his and *Jagdgeschwader* 52's last victory of the war. It is 8 May 1945, VE-Day in Europe, and Hartmann is on his 1405th combat mission. His orders – to locate the spearheads of the advancing Red Army. He has found them around the town of Brünn (Brno), in Czechoslovakia. And now, with the morning sun glinting on his canopy, and with his 352nd kill (an unidentified Soviet Yak fighter) going down in flames in his wake, Hartmann breaks away to lead his wingman back to base for one last landing.

There is still a great deal of controversy about both the actual aircraft Erich Hartmann was flying on this mission, and the markings it carried. At least one official document states quite categorically that JG 52 was equipped entirely with the Bf 109G-14 (of various models), and was earmarked for conversion to K-4s 'as soon as the logistical situation permits'. But the *Geschwader* is known to have operated a mix of G-14s and G-10s, and Hartmann himself spoke of flying both variants.

As to the vexed subject of the distinctive black 'tulip leaf' decoration applied to the nose of most of 'Bubi' Hartmann's later machines, many doubt that there would have been the time, or the inclination, to keep up this practice during the chaotic closing days of the war. But there are at least two known photographs of what are, undeniably, the remains of a K-4 amongst the wreckage abandoned at Deutsch-Brod carrying this self-same decoration. Whether Hartmann flew this particular aircraft is still open to question. The fact that the 'tulip leaf' motif itself survived until the very end is not

First published in Great Britain in 2004 by Osprey Publishing, Midland House, West Way, Botley, Oxford OX2 0PH, UK
443 Park Avenue South, New York, NY 10016, USA

ISBN 1 84176 786 7
A CIP catalogue record for this book is available from the British Library

Edited by Tony Holmes
Page design by Mark Holt
Cover Artwork by Mark Postlethwaite
Aircraft Profiles by John Weal
Index by Alan Thatcher

Printed in Hong Kong

05 06 07 08   10 9 8 7 6 5 4 3 2

EDITOR'S NOTE
To make this series as authoritative as possible, the Editor would be interested in hearing from any individual who may have relevant photographs, documentation or first-hand experiences relating to the world's elite units, their pilots and their aircraft of the various theatres of war. Any material used will be credited to its original source. Please contact Tony Holmes via e-mail at: tony.holmes@osprey-jets.freeserve.co.uk

ACKNOWLEDGEMENTS
The author would like to thank the following individuals for their generous help in providing photographs, documents and information.
In England – Chris Goss, Dr Alfred Price and Robert Simpson.
In Germany – Herren Wilhelm Deckers, Manfred Griehl, Walter Matthiesen, the late Heinz J Nowarra, Axel Paul, Günther Rall (Generalleutnant a.D.) and Karlheinz Wichmann.

CONTENTS

FROM SMALL BEGINNINGS

There are various ways of assessing the performance and effectiveness of a fighter unit. One famous fighter group is rightly proud of the fact that it did not lose a single one of its charges while engaged on bomber escort duties. Others can point with equal pride to their outstanding serviceability records, always being able to mount a maximum effort whenever called upon. Yet others can boast of completing operational tours with a minimum of combat casualties and exemplary kill-to-loss ratios.

But the commonest and most widely accepted measure of a fighter unit's success is the number of enemy machines it has shot down. And if this, admittedly rather simplistic, yardstick is applied, then one fighter formation towers head and shoulders above all the rest.

With well over 10,000 Allied aircraft destroyed during the course of World War 2, the Luftwaffe's *Jagdgeschwader* 52 established a record not only unsurpassed in the annals of military aviation history to date, but one which seems likely to stand for all time.

Beyond the relatively narrow confines of the air war historian and enthusiast, however, the designation JG 52 remains little known. This may be due partly to the fact that the unit was never honoured with a title, or even given a popular name. The pilots of JG 52 were no 'Richthofen Circus' or 'Abbeville Boys'. Nor, for some reason, did their 'Winged Sword' emblem enjoy the same widespread public recognition as, for example, JG 53's 'Ace-of-Spades' insignia.

But the main reason for the general lack of acclaim accorded to this, the most successful fighter unit in the world, undoubtedly lies in the fact that for some two-thirds of its entire existence, JG 52 operated exclusively on the eastern front.

Many of its actions were fought over the vast, often tractless wastes of the Russian steppe, or above obscure villages and hamlets whose names are to be found on no modern map. And by far the overwhelming majority of its victims were machines hacked from the amorphous, and to this day still largely anonymous, ranks of the wartime Red Air Force.

Had JG 52 been employed on Reich's Defence duties over cities such as Berlin, Hamburg or Cologne, or had it defended western European airspace against incursions from some of the better known and more widely publicised RAF and USAAF fighter units and aces, then its story would no doubt have been very different indeed. But JG 52's history does at least have its roots in the west.

It began in November 1938 with the activation of a single *Jagdgruppe* at Ingolstadt-Manching, an airfield some 37 miles (60 km) due north of Munich. As its designation indicated, I./JG 433 was the first *Gruppe* of the fourth single-seat *Jagdgeschwader* to be formed within the area controlled by *Luftwaffengruppenkommando* 3 – the territorial command which covered all of southern Germany.

The officer selected to lead the *Gruppe* was Hauptmann Dietrich Graf von Pfeil und Klein-Ellguth, who had commanded the provisional *Fliegergruppe* 10 during the Sudeten affair two months earlier.

The general easing of political tension throughout Europe in the immediate aftermath of the Sudeten crisis (which had been resolved by the signing of the Munich Agreement on 30 September 1938) was reflected in the slow, almost leisurely build-up of von Pfeil's new *Gruppe*. Although practically a full complement of Bf 109Ds was delivered to Ingolstadt during December, less than a dozen pilots had been posted in by year-end.

This discrepancy in numbers became academic when a spell of unexpectedly severe weather descended on much of Bavaria during the Christmas period. Housed in two unheated hangars, nearly every single one of the *Gruppe's* fighters was reportedly rendered unserviceable with their carburettor casings cracked as a result of the sharp overnight frosts.

Aircraft serviceability, and the weather, gradually improved during the opening weeks of 1939. New pilot intakes arrived fresh from training schools, and to assimilate these tyros and weld them into a cohesive whole von Pfeil was particularly fortunate in his appointed *Staffelkapitäne*, all three of whom were experienced veterans of the *Legion Condor*. 2. and

When first activated in 1938, I./JG 433 was initially equipped with Bf 109D-1s. This example provides a handy perch for a fully kitted-up Oberleutnant Lothar Ehrlich. Appointed *Staffelkapitän* of 8./JG 52 on 1 March 1940, Ehrlich was shot down off Margate on the opening day of III. *Gruppe's* disastrous participation in the Battle of Britain

7

Another founder-member of I./JG 433, Hauptmann Wolfgang Ewald served as *Kapitän* of 2. *Staffel* for almost 22 months before assuming command of I./JG 52 in August 1940. He is seen here as a major, wearing the Knight's Cross awarded to him in 1942 when *Gruppenkommandeur* of III./JG 3 on the eastern front

3./JG 433 were commanded by Oberleutnants Wolfgang Ewald and Alfons Klein, respectively (each with a single victory claimed in Spain).

Heading 1. *Staffel*, von Pfeil's senior *Kapitän* was a certain Oberleutnant Adolf Galland. A flyer with a passion for fighters, Galland had been forced to spend his recent tour with the *Legion* leading a ground-attack unit equipped with Heinkel He 51 biplanes (see Osprey *Elite Units 13 - Luftwaffe Schlachtgruppen* for further details). Returning from Spain, he had then been ordered to help organise the *ad hoc* ground-attack force being readied for possible action against the Czechs in the disputed Sudetenland. It was not until his subsequent posting to I./JG 433, effective as of 1 November 1938, that Adolf Galland felt he was at last back where he truly belonged – at the controls of the Luftwaffe's most advanced single-seat fighter.

On 18 February 1939 the *Gruppe*, still not yet at full strength, was dealt a tragic blow. While *en route* from Ingolstadt to Berlin, the unit's transport Ju 52/3m encountered a snowstorm over the Eger hills and crashed due to severe icing. All 11 occupants, passengers and crew, lost their lives. Among the dead was Oberleutnant Alfons Klein, who had purportedly hitched a lift on the ill-fated flight in order to visit the Berlin Motor Show.

For the next ten days 3./JG 433 operated under the caretaker leadership of Oberleutnant Karl-Heinz Leesmann until the arrival of Klein's official replacement on 1 March. Like his unfortunate predecessor, Oberleutnant Helmut Kühle was also an ex-member of the *Legion Condor*.

March was to witness a number of other changes. Two further intakes of newly qualified pilots finally brought the *Gruppe* up to full establishment. The unit also took delivery of its first Bf 109Es (although it would not relinquish the last of its venerable *Doras* until July). And towards the end of the month moves were put in hand to transfer I./JG 433 to its new permanent station.

Situated a few miles to the south-west of Stuttgart, the grass airfield at Böblingen was then serving as that city's main commercial airport (today's Echterdingen was still in the throes of construction). Upon taking up residence, von Pfeil's pilots would thus find themselves initially sharing the immediate airspace with the Ju 52/3ms and He 70s of Deutsche Lufthansa, as well as with other civilian traffic, both domestic and foreign. It was not an altogether ideal arrangement, but it *was* indicative of the way the Third Reich's rapidly expanding military air arm was outstripping the ground facilities provided for it.

On 13 April 1939 the *Gruppe* celebrated its arrival in its new 'home town' with due pomp and ceremony. While Hauptmann Dietrich Graf von Pfeil led a parade through the streets of Böblingen, the unit's Bf 109s staged an impressive fly-past low overhead. Some sources indicate, however, that the aerial components did not in fact vacate Ingolstadt until 20 April, when at least one *Staffel* (Adolf Galland's 1./JG 433) dog-legged to Böblingen by way of Munich, where it participated in another fly-past, this time in honour of the Führer's 50th birthday.

It was while the *Gruppe* was still settling in at Böblingen, on 1 May 1939 that the new and much-simplified system of block designations was introduced throughout most of the Luftwaffe. Henceforth, all fighter units stationed within the area controlled by *Luftflotte* 3 (as *Luftwaffen-gruppenkommando* (*Lw.Gr.Kdo.*) 3 had itself been redesignated) would be identified sequentially by numbers in the block 51-75. And whereas I./JG 433 had been in fourth (and last) position in *Lw.Gr.Kdo.* 3's single-seat fighter hierarchy, they were, for some reason, moved up two places during the re-numbering process to emerge as I./JG 52.

The ensuing summer months were taken up by a constant round of exercises and manoeuvres, both local – on one occasion I./JG 52 was tasked with defending nearby Stuttgart against an 'enemy' bomber fleet – and further afield.

In June the *Gruppe* was ordered to carry out a transfer to Wengerohr, a small field on the northern slopes of the Mosel (Moselle) valley. Hauptmann von Pfeil's unit may have been up to full strength in terms of aircraft and pilots, but it was still sadly lacking in many support services – as the current exercise proved. The move by road to Wengerohr was only made possible by the requisitioning of a large number of civilian lorries and their drivers.

Nor did the *Gruppe's* difficulties end there, for Wengerohr's grassy surface was softer and more uneven than Böblingen's hard-packed earth. There was a spate of minor take-off and landing accidents during I./JG 52's brief occupancy of the field, but fortunately no serious injuries to personnel.

The expedition to Wengerohr had obviously been designed to give von Pfeil's pilots and groundcrews a taste of operating on a war footing. The short-lived euphoria which had followed in the wake of the Munich Agreement had long since dissipated. In March 1939 Hitler's forces had occupied the rest of Czechoslovakia. Now it was adopting an increasingly threatening posture towards Poland. The Western Allies' policy of appeasement – so desperately held (and so dearly bought, at the expense of others) in the past – had proven totally ineffective. War clouds were looming large, and the threat of hostilities was becoming more real with every passing day.

Among the many signs of the heightened tension in what were to prove to be the final weeks of peace was the hurried activation of a number of makeshift fighter units of *Gruppe* or *Staffel* strength. One of these was 11.(N)/JG 72 – an auxiliary nightfighter *Staffel* equipped with elderly

Routine patrols did not always end routinely. For whatever reason, the unknown pilot of I./JG 52's 'White 7' has pulled off a very neat belly landing, with the only apparent damage to his Bf 109E being a set of bent propeller blades

Arado Ar 68F biplanes. Commanded by Oberleutnant August-Wilhelm Schumann, it was activated at Böblingen alongside I./JG 52 on 15 July 1939.

On a more personal level, another minor, but significant, portent of things to come was the departure of a thoroughly disgruntled Adolf Galland. On 31 July he was posted back to the ground-attack arm, where he assumed command of 5.(Schl)/LG 2 – the Heinkel He 51 *Staffel* he would lead into action in the imminent campaign against Poland. His place at the head of 1./JG 52 was taken by Oberleutnant Wilhelm Keidel.

The *Gruppe's* last pre-war deployment was to Wangerooge, one of the Friesian islands off the northern coast of Germany above Wilhelmshaven. Here, pilots spent two weeks honing their dogfighting skills and perfecting their gunnery. An RAF fighter pilot who underwent a similar experience off the English coast was later famously to remark, after being ordered to fire at the wave tops, 'The North Sea wasn't all that difficult to hit!'

But as well as stalking and shooting at the shadows of each others' aircraft as they raced across the sun-dappled surface of the water, von Pfeil's pilots also enjoyed the additional luxury of a target drogue, towed by an ancient Junkers F 13, which they used to simulate beam attacks on enemy bombers. The pilots put in about two hours of hard flying every day, after which their time was pretty much their own. It did not take them long to discover the delights that the unspoilt holiday island of Wangerooge had to offer.

All too soon, however, it was back to business as usual. Shortly after I./JG 52's return to Böblingen in mid-August 1939, full mobilisation was ordered. Reservists were recalled, and the *Gruppe* prepared itself for the task of defending the Stuttgart area, and its many manufacturing plants – including the important Mercedes motor works – from possible bombing raids by the French.

Then, on 26 August, the *Gruppe* was suddenly ordered to move up to Bonn-Hangelar. I./JG 52's new role in the – now seemingly inevitable – event of hostilities was to be the aerial defence of the southern flank of the industrial Ruhr basin.

When von Pfeil's pilots finally departed Böblingen on 29 August (just 72 hours prior to Hitler's invasion of Poland), they left behind their last remaining Bf 109Ds. These were then used to re-equip Oberleutnant August-Wilhelm Schumann's 11.(N)/JG 72.

On that same date, 11.(N)/JG 72 was joined at Böblingen by another of the *Staffeln* hastily formed during the last weeks of peace. Activated as a day-fighter unit at Schleissheim in mid-July, 1./JG 71 had flirted briefly with ex-Czech air force Avia B 534s, before itself quickly converting to the Bf 109D. By an odd coincidence, 1./JG 71 was also commanded by a Schumann – Oberleutnant Heinz Schumann.

It was intended that the two Böblingen-based *Staffeln* (11./JG 72 having been relieved of its quasi-nocturnal duties) should form two-thirds the strength of the planned new II./JG 52. In the event, the outbreak of hostilities on 1 September seems to have put the creation of a second *Gruppe* temporarily on hold. For the first fortnight of the war, the two *Staffeln* operated in a kind of administrative limbo. Some sources refer to 1./JG 71 and 11./JG 72 as the 4. and 5. *Staffeln* respectively of the embryonic II./JG 52. The units themselves appear to have continued using their original designations. Given the common name shared by the two *Staffelkapitäne*, others got round the problem quite simply by referring to the pair collectively as the '*Jagdgruppe* Schumann'!

Plans had also been drawn up in the third week of August 1939 for the establishment at Böblingen of a *Geschwaderstab* JG 52 to be commanded by Major Hubert Merhart von Bernegg, hitherto *Gruppenkommandeur* of II./JG 53. But these too appear to have been perforce delayed by the attack on Poland. It was not until the latter half of September that Major von Bernegg's *Stab* took its place as part of the *Westwall* defences – by which time Great Britain and France had declared war on Germany, and the first clashes between the Luftwaffe and the *Armée de l'Air* had already taken place.

SITZKRIEG

The invasion of Poland was some 54 hours old when first the British, and then the French, declarations of war on Germany were announced on 3 September 1939. The ensuing autumn and winter months have since been dismissed by many as the *Sitzkrieg*, or Phoney War.

There was more than a grain of truth in these somewhat derogatory terms as far as ground operations were concerned. The majority of French and German troops sat phlegmatically in their respective fortifications, each side waiting for the other to make its move. Members of the newly arrived British Expeditionary Force (BEF) complained that they were spending more time labouring than soldiering, as they dug earthworks and poured concrete along the Belgian border.

But in the air it was a different story. Weather permitting, both sides mounted fighter patrols and sent up reconnaissance sorties to probe and gauge each other's defences. Such activity was mainly local, however, and contact with the enemy was at first the exception rather than the rule.

Although taken in the spring of 1940, this snapshot captures perfectly the sense of boredom felt throughout much of the *Sitzkrieg* period. Whiling away the time in front of I. *Gruppe's* ops hut, Oberleutnant Carl Lommel, *Kapitän* of 1. *Staffel*, is engrossed in a newspaper. Behind him, Leutnant Robert Göbel appears more interested in the shine on his boots! As *Staffelkapitän* of 2./JG 52 in Russia, Oberleutnant Göbel would be killed in a Soviet night bombing raid on the unit's forward landing ground at Grakovo on 25 June 1942

At Bonn-Hangelar, for example, I./JG 52 had little to show for its first month of routine border patrolling.

It thus fell to the *'Jagdgruppe* Schumann' at Böblingen – or, more specifically, to Leutnant Paul Gutbrod of 11./JG 72 – to score the very first of the more than 10,000 aerial victories which would be credited to JG 52 before the final German surrender six years hence.

On the evening of 6 September, Leutnant Gutbrod and his wingman were patrolling the Rhine south of Karlsruhe when they spotted a 'high-winged monoplane' apparently attempting to strafe the bridge at Kehl. As soon as it became aware of the approaching fighters, the enemy machine – a two-seater Mureaux ANF 115 reconnaissance aircraft – broke off and headed back towards the French side of the river. Before it could escape, Gutbrod was able to get in two firing passes from astern, the second of which caused the Mureaux to break up in mid-air.

This hapless Frenchman (ANF 115 No 14 of the Sarrebourg-based GAO 553) was not just the opening entry on JG 52's previously virgin scoresheet, it also provided the Luftwaffe with its first western front aerial victory of the war.

Four weeks to the day after Leutnant Gutbrod's success – which had earned him the Iron Cross, 2nd Class – it was the turn of I./JG 52 to claim another French reconnaissance intruder.

Shortly after midday on 6 October, one of the first of the *Armée de l'Air's* brand new LeO 451 twin-engined bombers was ordered to carry out a

When 1./JG 71 became 4./JG 52 and swapped its Avia B 534s for Bf 109s, it introduced a new *Staffel* badge. In place of the 'winged red devil', which had adorned the rear fuselages of the ex-Czech air force biplanes, the unit now opted for a black arched cat – either on a soft-sprayed background as here, or on a solid white disc. And while on the subject of white, note the unknown pilot's fetching pre-war flying helmet!

Occasionally – very occasionally – the tranquility of the *Sitzkrieg* would be shattered by contact with the enemy, and then a kill. This happened just twice to I./JG 52. The first time was on 6 October 1939 when 2. *Staffel's* Leutnant Hans Berthel chased and destroyed a French Leo 451 . . .

hazardous solo reconnaissance mission deep into German airspace to gather intelligence on Luftwaffe defences south of the Ruhr. It was against just such an eventuality that I./JG 52 had been transferred up to Bonn-Hangelar. And it was also the reason why the *Gruppe* – in addition to its frequent patrols – kept at least one *Schwarm* of (four) fighters at constant cockpit readiness.

In the event, when the first reports of the lone intruder began to come in from the ground observers, two *Schwärme* were immediately scrambled to intercept it. One of the eight pilots, Leutnant Hans Berthel – who had occupied the No 9 slot in Germany's pre-war national aerobatic team, and now regularly flew as wingman to Oberleutnant Wolfgang Ewald, *Staffelkapitän* of 2./JG 52 – takes up the story (translated from the original German by kind permission of Herr Axel Paul, co-author of *Vom Feindflug nicht zurückgekehrt* – see bibliography);

'I was reputed to have the best eyes in the *Staffel*. After we had been flying a little while, I was therefore the first – well before my comrades –

... seen here burning furiously after attempting a wheels-down landing in a field near Wachendorf, south-west of Bonn. After rescuing the injured crew, the onlookers (background left) at first kept a respectful distance from the blazing machine . . .

to spot the tiny speck of an aircraft in the far distance. It wasn't long before I was able to identify it as a French LeO 451 bomber. I reported the fact over the R/T, but my sighting was received with some scepticism. I discovered later that none of my comrades had believed me!

'All of us, friend and foe alike, were flying between two layers of cloud. The Frenchman was also on the ball, and he caught sight of me as soon as I curved in towards him. The pilot immediately put his nose down and went into a steep dive, trying to reach the protection of the lower cloud layer. I decided to follow him down, even if it did mean flying blind, for which my "Red 1" was not equipped.

'Luckily, I did not have to fly blind for long. When I broke through the cloud and had clear visibility again, I was absolutely amazed to find the Frenchman almost right in front of me, just off to one side. We were, at most, 100 metres (330 ft) above the fields flashing past beneath us.

'The enemy rear-gunner spotted me at once and quickly opened fire. Fortunately, he did not hit me – I say fortunately because in all the excitement – it was, after all, the first time I had ever *seen* the enemy,

. . . but later approached the still smouldering wreckage to pick over the pieces . . .

. . . among the items retrieved was the LeO's port rudder, which made a very nice trophy for the *Staffel's* Kasino (officers' mess) . . .

. . . while outside in its wooded dispersal pen, Berthel's 'Red 1' was decorated with the unit's very first victory bar

let alone finding myself being shot at – I was frantically pushing and pulling every available button and lever in the cockpit in an effort to release the safety catches and charge my guns. In the process, I even managed to switch my lights on. They remained on until I landed, leading to the usual witty remarks from my comrades for a long time afterwards.

'In reality, it can only have been a matter of seconds until my guns were ready to fire, although at the time it seemed like an eternity.

'My first burst of fire hit one of the Frenchman's engines, which immediately burst into flames. The pilot of the LeO promptly lowered his undercarriage – a somewhat unusual and dangerous move to make prior to an emergency landing. In this instance, it was particularly dangerous for me! The undercarriage immediately broke up on contact with the soft ground. Bits and pieces flew through the air, missing my "Red 1" by a hair's breadth as – with my excess of speed – I zoomed low across the path of the careering Frenchman. What would have happened if the wheel that narrowly missed my cockpit had actually hit me? Even if it had only resulted in a slight dent, it would have taken a long while to live down the inevitable jokes from my comrades.

'By chance, Major Gotthard Handrick, winner of the modern pentathlon in the 1936 Berlin Olympics and himself a fighter pilot (currently *Gruppenkommandeur* of I./JG 26, based at Bonn-Odendorf) happened to be in Wachendorf (17 miles (28 km) southwest of Bonn) at the time. Alerted by the loud noise of the engines, he had witnessed the combat from the ground. He officially confirmed the kill, or at least later described the whole event – including the LeO's emergency landing – to my own *Kommandeur*.

'I remained on the scene for some time, orbiting and watching the burning French machine. Then my circling was abruptly terminated by a radio message. Control was reporting the presence of several English fighters over the Eifel hills. Fired up by the spirit of the chase, we turned on to the given heading and set off to find the *Engländer*. But we could discover no trace of them and, after spending some time searching, returned to Hangelar.'

By this first week of October 1939, Maj von Bernegg's *Geschwaderstab* and the new II./JG 52 were both fully established at Böblingen on Bf 109Es. The latter, commanded by Hauptmann Horst-Günter von Kornatzki (later to achieve fame as the originator of the *Sturmjäger* concept), had been brought up to full strength by the activation of a 6. *Staffel*, headed by Oberleutnant Werner Lederer. Meanwhile, any lingering confusion surrounding the common surname shared by the *Kapitäne* of 4. and 5./JG 52 was overcome by referring to the pair, informally at least, in terms best translated as 'Lofty' Schumann and 'Shorty' Schumann, respectively!

Exactly a week after Hans Berthel's LeO 451 victory, Leutnant Kurt Kirchner of 1./JG 52 claimed I. *Gruppe's* second, and last, success of the *Sitzkrieg* period. His victim would also prove to be the sole RAF machine downed by JG 52 prior to the invasion of France the following spring. It was one of a trio of Blenheim IVs from No 114 Sqn despatched on 12 October from their home base at Wyton, in the UK, to Villeneuve les Vertus, east of Paris, which currently housed the Fairey Battles of No 105 Sqn. From here, the Blenheims were to participate in a special long-range reconnaissance effort scheduled for the following day. Flying singly, they crossed the German border south of Luxembourg, before wheeling northwards in a wide arc to exit enemy airspace out over the North Sea.

Plt Off K G S Thompson in Blenheim N6160 was destined never to make it. His aircraft was reportedly intercepted by a *Schwarm* of I./JG 52 fighters shortly after crossing the frontier. Reference sources differ, however, as to the machine's precise fate. Some state that it came down shortly after contact was made over the Idar-Oberstein area east-southeast of Trier, while others maintain that it crashed near Duisburg after having covered a good half of its intended path through hostile territory.

On 27 October the *Geschwaderstab* and II./JG 52 transferred northwards from Böblingen to Mannheim – another of Germany's pre-war international civil airports now housing military units.

Less than a fortnight after this move, on 8 November, II. *Gruppe* scored its first two 'official' victories (discounting the Mureaux claimed by 11./JG 72's Leutnant Paul Gutbrod exactly two months presviously). In the early afternoon Oberleutnant Heinz Schumann, *Staffelkapitän* of 4./JG 52, downed a French observation balloon west of the Rhine opposite Karlsruhe. Some 90 minutes later, and 25 miles (40 km) further to the west, 5./JG 52's Leutnant Karl Faust added a Morane MS 406 to the *Gruppe's* scoreboard after a brief dogfight near Bitche.

If the first of this day's two successes seems less than heroic, it should be borne in mind that the sites of the tethered observation balloons were nearly always ringed by heavy anti-aircraft defences, and their destruction was regarded as a valuable and noteworthy achievement. The risks involved are underlined by the fact that the downing of such a manned balloon – as opposed to an undefended balloon forming part of an aerial barrage – was officially recognised as being on a par with the shooting down of an enemy aircraft.

Throughout November the Luftwaffe was still trying to introduce some semblance of order among the miscellany of fighter units it had hurriedly thrust into the *Westwall* positions upon the outbreak of war two months earlier. Now, with the campaign in Poland long won and his eastern frontiers secure – and with the onset of winter weather precluding any major action in the west – Hitler was intent upon reorganising and building up the western front orders of battle in preparation for his intended spring offensive.

Among November's moves was the transfer of I./JG 52 back down from Bonn-Hangelar (where it had operated as part of the northern sector's *Luftflotte* 2, and had been subordinated to the *Stäbe* of both JGs 26 and 77) to Lachen-Speyerdorf. Here, for the first time, it came under the control of its own parent *Stab* JG 52 at nearby Mannheim, which formed part of *Luftflotte* 3, whose forces were arrayed in the south along the Franco-German border.

On 21 November, six days after the *Gruppe's* arrival at Lachen-Speyerdorf, Hauptmann Dietrich Graf von Pfeil und Klein-Ellguth celebrated his 32nd birthday. The occasion was marked by a small gathering in the officers' mess, where toasts were drunk and a set of small silver goblets was presented to him. Afterwards, Hauptmann von Pfeil announced that he intended to fly a routine patrol in the company of his *Gruppen*-Adjutant, Leutnant Christoph Geller. It was a fateful decision.

Unlike II./JG 52, which had opted for three separate *Staffel* badges but had no *Gruppe* emblem, I./JG 52 selected a communal device for use on all its machines. The design chosen – a running boar – is seen here on the cowling of Oberleutnant Lommel's 'White 1'. The pilots are trying to persuade a black cat to sit on the cowling alongside the unit badge, but the reluctant feline is having none of it. All the photographers get for their pains is a black blur as the cat leaps to the ground

Heading west, the two Messerschmitts were bounced by half-a-dozen *Armée de l'Air* Curtiss Hawk H-75As flying a high-level sweep along the French border. The *Kommandeur's* machine immediately went down in flames, crashing east of Pirmasens, just inside German territory. Although he managed to bale out, von Pfeil suffered grievous burns. Despite his aircraft being damaged, Leutnant Geller was able to escape, and he attempted to get back to Lachen-Speyerdorf, only to come down some six miles (10 km) short of the field.

Von Pfeil's injuries were so severe that they ended his flying career, and it was nearly two years before he was able to return to duty. A succession of ground appointments culminated in his assuming command of 4.*Jagd-Division* in France shortly before the invasion of Normandy. Oberstleutnant von Pfeil's car was ambushed by members of the French resistance on 14 July 1944. Seriously wounded a second time, he died in hospital at Verdun.

For JG 52, as for many other units stationed along the *Westwall*, the worsening weather meant a marked reduction in aerial activity. This would last throughout the depths of one of the harshest winters the region had known for many years. In fact, operations were so limited during this period that it was apparently not deemed necessary to bring in an official successor to Hauptmann von Pfeil for very nearly three months. Instead, Oberleutnant Wolfgang Ewald, *Staffelkapitän* of 2./JG 52, was ordered to take on the additional duties of acting *Gruppenkommandeur* at Lachen-Speyerdorf.

The day after he did so, on 22 November, a member of Ewald's 2.*Staffel* had the dubious distinction of becoming JG 52's first operational fatality. While on a high-altitude patrol of the border, Unteroffizier

17

For the first six months of its existence, the new III./JG 52 wore no unit badges at all. It did, however, display the oversized wavy bar III. *Gruppe* symbol (which would become its trademark) from the very outset. It is modelled here by an embarrassed-looking 'Black 10', down on one knee after suffering starboard undercarriage failure at Mannheim in April 1940

This shot of Unteroffizier Leo Zaunbrecher (left), the pilot credited with the Potez 63 south of Zweibrücken, offers a first glimpse of 5. *Staffel's* 'little red devil' badge. Note too the dark overalls worn by Zaunbrecher's chief mechanic on the right – a perfect illustration of why groundcrews were referred to as *'schwarze Männer'* ('black men') in common Luftwaffe parlance

Hans-Joachim Hellwig's 'Red 4' suddenly, and inexplicably, went into a steep dive, crashing behind the French lines. His loss was subsequently attributed to a malfunction in the aircraft's oxygen system.

A similar dearth of activity during the winter months of 1939-40 was also afflicting II./JG 52 at nearby Mannheim. With little to occupy it by day, one report even suggests that the High Command ordered 5. *Staffel* (the ex-11.(N)/JG 72) to revert to its original nightfighting role. To this end, a dozen elderly He 51 biplanes were delivered to the *Staffel*, together with instructions to begin conversion at once.

'Shorty' Schumann's protests at this indignity were long and loud. So vociferous were his complaints that the *Staffel* was eventually allowed to keep its Bf 109s – but the Heinkels stayed too. There then arose the curious situation of a unit operating Bf 109s by day and He 51s by night! This allegedly went on for about two months, with the Heinkels only being flown on bright, moonlit nights.

Whatever the truth behind this story, one thing is certain. When II./JG 52 made the short hop from Mannheim to its new base at Speyer (ten miles (16 km) to the south) on 1 February 1940, the *Gruppe* was equipped solely with Bf 109s. Any He 51s which may, or may not, have been foisted upon 5. *Staffel* had been left behind with no tears shed.

February was to witness a resumption of the preparations for the planned assault on France. On 9 February Hauptmann Siegfried von Eschwege, *Geschwader*-Adjutant of JG 52, who had been named as Hauptmann von Pfeil's replacement shortly after the latter's wounding on 21 November, officially took up office as the *Gruppenkommandeur* of I./JG 52.

Then, towards the end of February, I. and II./JG 52 were each ordered to relinquish part of their strengths in both men and equipment to assist in the formation of a III. *Gruppe*.

This unit, under the command of Major Wolf-Heinrich von Houwald (erstwhile *Staffelkapitän* of 3./JG 26), was activated at Strausberg – an airfield some 17 miles (28 km) to the east of Berlin – on 1 March 1940. Ably assisted by his three *Staffelkapitäne*, Oberleutnants Herbert Fermer, Lothar Ehrlich and Karl Plunser (of 7., 8. and 9./JG 52 respectively), Major von Houwald set about the task of transforming his fledgling *Gruppe* into a cohesive fighting force as quickly as possible. After nearly six weeks at Strausberg, III./JG 52 was transferred to Mannheim-Sandhofen on 6 April to continue the working-up process under the supervision of *Stab* JG 53.

While III./JG 52 was training at Strausberg, the two *Gruppen* based along the *Westwall* had managed to add just one more enemy aircraft to the *Geschwader's* still less than impressive collective total. On 24 March a *Schwarm* of 5. *Staffel* machines patrolling west of Pirmasens intercepted a French reconnaissance Potez 637 over Zweibrücken. Unteroffiziere Leo Zaunbrecher and Albert Griener shared in its destruction, although it was the former alone who was officially credited with the kill.

JG 52's six victories of the Phoney War period had been achieved without the Geschwader suffering a single combat fatality. The only loss of life to date had been that of I. *Gruppe's* Unteroffizier Hellwig. But in the space of the next month both II. and III. *Gruppen* would each lose a pilot in collisions – one during take-off and the other in a mid-air collision.

One of the last aerial encounters involving aircraft of JG 52 to take place before the now imminent invasion of France occurred shortly after midday on 23 April. On that date a dozen machines of I. *Gruppe* escorted one of their own reconnaissance Do 17Ps (of 1.(H)/13) across the French frontier near Saarbrücken. When east of Metz, some 20 miles (32 km) inside enemy territory, the formation was intercepted by ten Hawk H-75As. Five of the French fighters went after the Dornier, while the others waded into the Messerschmitts. In the melée, machines on both sides suffered damage. Two of the Bf 109s were hit and turned back for the border trailing smoke. One only just made it, a wounded Oberfeldwebel Franz Essl of 2. *Staffel* pulling off a successful crash-landing immediately behind the German lines.

Essl was JG 52's final casualty of the *Sitzkrieg* sparring. Less than three weeks later Hitler would launch his all-out assault on France and the Low Countries. The Phoney War was over and the real war was about to begin.

The *Geschwader's* six Phoney War victories were very much the exception rather than the rule. The period ended as it had begun with long hours of inactivity, as demonstrated here by 1. *Staffel's* pilots on a balmy April day at Lachen-Speyerdorf. Lounging in the deckchairs in the foreground are Leutnants Robert Göbel (left) and Günther Büsgen. Behind them, doing a spot of gardening, are Oberfeldwebel Oskar Strack (in shirt sleeve order) and Feldwebel Herbert Bischoff. Strack would be reported missing over the Channel on 26 October 1940. Bischoff and Büsgen were but two of the 28(!) pilots of JG 52 to become PoWs during the Battle of Britain. This photograph offers a wealth of detail to the dedicated diorama modeller. Note the air-raid siren on the roof of the ops hut to the right, and the vehicle park (including a truck, ambulance and staff car) on the hardstanding behind it. Also of interest are the tripod-mounted periscopic binoculars to the left of the group, the loudspeakers slung from the telegraph poles and the solitary Bf 109 parked out on the field beyond

FRONTFLIEGER IM WESTEN

The *Blitzkrieg* in the west, launched in the early hours of 10 May 1940, found the units of JG 52 stationed together in and around Mannheim. But they were not operating as a single formation. While Major von Bernegg's *Geschwaderstab*, together with I. and II./JG 52, formed part of V. *Fliegerkorps*, and were tasked with securing the airspace above the left flank of Army Group A (the middle of the three Army Groups lined up against the Western allies), the as-yet untested III. *Gruppe* remained under the control of JG 53, and was charged with border defence duties.

The campaign began with the now famous 'feint' on the far northern flank through the Low Countries. While this was having the desired effect of luring the British and French out of their entrenched positions (those earthworks so laboriously dug during the autumn and winter months!) and forward into Belgium, the units of the real striking force – including the Panzer divisions of Army Group A – were kept hidden in the wooded valleys of the Ardennes awaiting the right moment to exploit the breach opening up in front of them.

For von Bernegg's pilots the first four days of the *Blitzkrieg* were therefore relatively uneventful. Several patrols clashed with their French

What a difference a month makes! Four of the pilots seen in the final photograph of the previous chapter are pictured here, still at Lachen-Speyerdorf, after flying their first mission of the French campaign on the morning of 10 May 1940. Although the patrol proved uneventful, the quartet appear much more animated. They are, from left to right, Unteroffizier Reinhard Neumann, Feldwebel Bischoff, Feldwebel Heinz Uerlings and Oberfeldwebel Strack. Neumann was subsequently killed in a crash after I./JG 52's return to Germany in late June, while Uerlings belly-landed near Canterbury at the beginning of September to join Bischoff in British captivity

counterparts, but all such encounters proved inconclusive. It was not until the Panzers were unleashed to make their dash for the Meuse at Sedan, where crossings had to be secured before the armour could begin scything its way through north-eastern France to the Channel coast, that the air war on this central sector erupted in earnest.

14 May has since gone down in Luftwaffe folklore as the 'Day of the Fighters'. Suddenly realising the danger threatening to split their forces in two, British and French commanders threw every available bomber against the vital Meuse bridges in a day-long attempt to halt the advance of the Panzers. *Luftflotte* 3's fighters reacted strongly. By the time darkness fell, the remains of 89 Allied aircraft littered the floor of the Meuse valley.

Having moved up to Ober-Olm, near Mainz, 24 hours earlier – and from there staging via Wengerohr, above the Mosel, to bring themselves closer to the scene of the impending action – the pilots of Hauptmann von Kornatzki's II./JG 52 claimed a dozen enemy aircraft destroyed, including eight Fairey Battles. Among the victors were the two Schumanns, 'Lofty' getting a Battle to add to his observation balloon of the previous November, and 'Shorty' opening his score with a Bloch 210. The *Gruppe's* only casualty was Feldwebel Hans Bauer of 4. *Staffel*, who was killed when his 'White 4' somersaulted on landing back at Wengerohr.

I./JG 52 had also been ordered closer to the front on 13 May. Its move took the *Gruppe* to Hoppstädten, some 24 miles (38 km) southeast of Trier, which would be its base for the next eight days. During this time the unit undertook escort duties for V. *Fliegerkorps'* bombers attacking targets around Sedan, Verdun and beyond, as well as mounting *freie Jagd* sweeps along the Meuse. It was one of the latter, flown on 15 May, which resulted in the *Geschwader's* sole PoW of the French campaign. During a scrappy engagement with a clutch of MS 406s over Charleville, Leutnant Kurt

This somewhat damaged and out-of-focus shot (obviously snatched from the cockpit of the neighbouring machine) is nonetheless of interest for showing Oberleutnant August-Wilhelm Schumann's 'Black 1'. And could that be 'Shorty' Schumann himself (minus jacket) having a few words with three of his men? The latter's rigid posture, and the *Spiess* ('chiefy') marching purposefully away from the little group, suggest that perhaps all is not well

Kirchner was forced to take to his parachute behind enemy lines. His period in captivity was to be brief, however, for he was among the many prisoners released after the French Armistice the following month.

II./JG 52 had better fortune during its clash with MS 406s northwest of Charleville on that same 15 May, being able to claim four of the French fighters without loss. This brought the *Gruppe's* collective total to 19 confirmed kills, making it by far the most successful of JG 52's three *Gruppen* to date. But it did not prevent the unit from being recalled to Speyer 48 hours later for a brief stint of border defence duties.

It was now time for von Houwald's III./JG 52 to get in on the act. Still subordinated to *Stab* JG 53, the *Gruppe* was transferred up to Ippesheim, a forward landing ground southwest of Mainz, on 15 May. After three uneventful days, ten of their number were detailed to rendezvous with a He 111 returning from a reconnaissance mission over France and escort it safely back to Germany.

The Heinkel was found without difficulty, but south of Metz, while still 25 miles (40 km) inside French airspace, the formation was spotted by a dozen Hawk H-75As. The leutnant leading the second *Schwarm* of 8./JG 52 Messerschmitts clearly recalls what happened next;

'It was our first contact with the enemy. Everyone was tremendously excited, and we immediately forgot everything we'd ever learned. Tactics and radio discipline went out of the window. We were all shouting at once. I was bathed in sweat.'

Concentrating on the Heinkel, the Hawks were bounced by the higher-flying Bf 109s. A wild dogfight erupted – 'everyone tangled with everyone else' – during which the He 111 managed to escape. Nine of III. *Gruppe's* fighters also returned unscathed to Ippesheim (the tenth suffered slight damage on crash-landing with a punctured tyre). Three of the French Hawks had been shot down, with the leutnant who had described the action claiming to have scored hits on a fourth. But at debriefing, it transpired that his wingman, Leutnant Helmut Lössnitz, had seen the pilot of the fourth Hawk (reportedly a Czech NCO serving with the

These *Emils* of I./JG 52 were photographed during a stop-over at Mannheim-Sandhofen while *en route* to Hoppstädten in mid-May. Only about half of the machines seen here appear to be wearing the *Gruppe's* 'running boar' badge

Armée de l'Air) bale out of the stricken machine. The claim for an 'e/a damaged' was promptly upgraded to that of a confirmed kill. It was to be the first of many for the then Leutnant Günther Rall, who would go on to add 274 more to emerge, not only as one of JG 52's three highest scorers, but as the third most successful fighter pilot in history!

The week that followed was an eventful one. On 22 May the *Geschwaderstab* and II./JG 52 moved to Sandweiler. On the same date I. *Gruppe* flew in to Charleville, henceforth to operate – like III. *Gruppe* – under the control of JG 53. This left *Kommodore* Major von Bernegg with just II./JG 52. And it was the latter which, on 24 May, was to suffer the *Geschwader's* first combat fatality when 4. *Staffel's* Leutnant Martin Mund was shot down by Curtiss Hawks near Longwy.

Forty-eight hours later, having in the meantime transferred to Trier and added two more French aircraft to its scoreboard, III./JG 52 likewise lost a pilot to Curtiss Hawks. This second victim was Leutnant Helmut Planer of 9. *Staffel*, whose *Emil* went down near Diedenhofen.

Under a towering late spring sky, the *Emils* of III./JG 52 sit patiently at Trier-Euren, awaiting their next mission. During its two-week occupancy of Trier, III. *Gruppe* was able to claim two *Armée de l'Air* machines, but lost one of its own

After having moved up to Laon-Couvron the day before, it was also on 26 May that Hauptmann von Eschwege's I. *Gruppe* claimed its sole success of the French campaign – one of the *Armée de l'Air*'s seemingly ubiquitous Hawk H-75As, shot down over Chantilly by Feldwebel Alfons Bacher of 8./JG 52.

During its week at Laon-Couvron I./JG 52's fighters were deployed several times to Cambrai, which was used as a forward field for operations over the Dunkirk area. With the German plan to split the Allied armies in two having succeeded beyond all expectations, the BEF was now in full retreat, and attempting to extricate as much of its strength as possible from the harbour and beaches of Dunkirk.

The successful conclusion of the Dunkirk evacuation in the early hours of 3 June (in the space of little more than a week, some one-third of a million British and French troops had been transported safely back across the Channel), marked the end of Operation *Yellow*, the first part of Hitler's conquest of France. Now his forces were poised for the second phase – Operation *Red* – ready to wheel southwards and thrust through the bulk of the still intact French armies deep in the heart of France.

The involvement and fortunes of JG 52's component units differed considerably in this second act of the campaign. Among the many organisational changes made in preparation for the drive south was the release of both I. and III. *Gruppen* from the control of JG 53. But whereas the latter returned to the JG 52 fold upon its move from Trier to Hoppstädten on 1 June, Hauptmann von Eschwege's I./JG 52 was withdrawn from the front altogether and transferred to Zerbst, 62 miles (100 km) southwest of Berlin, to defend central Germany's industrial regions.

Meanwhile, the *Geschwaderstab* and II./JG 52 were to remain at Sandweiler, in Luxembourg. It was from here, on the afternoon of 1 June, that a *Rotte* (two machines) of the *Gruppenstab* II./JG 52 took off. Some sources describe it as an emergency scramble, others refer to the pair being despatched to locate and destroy a French observation balloon reported to be operating out of a clearing in the woods near Pouilly, south of Mouzon.

The formation leader was Oberleutnant Werner Gutowski and his wingman Oberleutnant Paul Gutbrod (the 11./JG 72 pilot who had destroyed the Mureaux ANF 115 in the opening week of the *Sitzkrieg*). Gutowski's subsequent account appears to corroborate the fact that the pair had indeed been sent out to find a balloon;

'We approached the bend in the Meuse near Pouilly, flying approximately 330 ft (100 m) apart below gathering heavy cloud. We circled the woods south of Pouilly a number of times, for some five to seven minutes in all, but there was no sign of a balloon.

'Beginning yet another circuit southwards from the centre of Pouilly, Oberleutnant Gutbrod's machine climbed slowly into the clouds. I followed him but, finding myself flying into a large storm cloud, dived back down to regain sight of the ground. This is when I lost all visual and radio contact with Oberleutnant Gutbrod.

'I immediately climbed back up through a hole in the clouds, but could not spot his machine above the layer either. I continued circling the area for about ten minutes – sometimes above, sometimes below the clouds – all the while trying to contact him on the R/T. But there was neither sight nor sound of him.

'Finally, assuming he had returned to base alone, and with my own fuel now running low, I broke off the search and also headed back to base.'

In fact, Oberleutnant Paul Gutbrod was to remain missing, his *Emil* having presumably crashed into the woods near Pouilly, possibly due to loss of orientation in the heavy, electrical storm clouds.

The primary task of Major von Bernegg's pilots in the second phase of the campaign against France remained, as before, the protection of Army Group A's left flank. But the Panzers' route of advance was no longer due west to the Channel coast. This time they were to push south-eastwards, down behind the now defunct Maginot Line, towards the Swiss frontier.

Operation *Red* was preceded by a major air attack on targets in the Greater Paris area on 3 June. Although only marginally involved in these

From Trier, III./JG 52 moved to Hoppstädten, where it was to spend the first week of June. Although picturesque, the field offered few facilities. The Bf 109s were parked alongside unfinished timber revetments . . .

. . . and the groundcrews were housed under canvas. While at Hoppstädten, the *Gruppe* added two more kills – a brace of Curtiss Hawks on 3 June – to its final tally of ten western front victories

operations, III./JG 52 did manage to claim a brace of Hawk H-75As near Reims on this date. Six days later another pair of French fighters – two Morane MS 406s downed in the vicinity of Réthel – provided the *Gruppe* with its last successes of the campaign.

Having briefly occupied three different French airfields in the space of a week, III./JG 52 was recalled to Hoppstädten on 13 June. Further transfers followed, including a stop-over in southern Germany, before the *Gruppe* was finally sent up to Jever, on the North Sea coast, in the closing days of the month.

Meanwhile, Hauptmann von Kornatzki's II./JG 52 had been upholding its lead as the most successful *Gruppe* in the *Geschwader*. For much of Operation *Red*, II./JG 52 remained firmly rooted at Sandweiler, in Luxembourg. All but one of the ten kills scored during this period were, however, claimed during a brief foray onto French soil.

The most successful day of all occurred midway through the *Gruppe's* five-day occupancy of Laon when, during the course of 9 June, it brought down five enemy aircraft in three separate engagements. The two victims of the late afternoon clash were reportedly RAF Hurricanes – the first, and

With 27 confirmed victories (including all ten of the RAF kills), II./JG 52 was by far the most successful of the *Geschwader's* three *Gruppen* during the campaign in France. 5. *Staffel* was credited with exactly one-third of this overall total. Here, 5./JG 52's Bf 109Es are seen occupying a windswept and apparently somewhat soggy dispersal (note the vehicle tracks) as they take a break between patrols

only, British machines to fall to JG 52 in France since the Fairey Battles claimed during the 'Day of the Fighters' nearly a month earlier.

Forty-eight hours later, and with two more French machines downed south of Reims, II./JG 52 was withdrawn from operations. Within a week the *Gruppe* had been ordered back to Karlsruhe, in Germany.

THE BATTLE OF BRITAIN

JG 52's role in the recent Battle of France may be described as having been peripheral at best. Although the same could not be said of the part it was to play in the forthcoming Battle of Britain, where it would find itself involved in the thick of the cross-Channel fighting, the *Geschwader's* presence and contribution to the Battle was, if anything, even more fragmentary.

For even after some 12 months of hostilities, during which time most *Jagdgeschwader* had established themselves on the Luftwaffe's orders of battle, it would appear that JG 52's individual *Gruppen* were still being used to carry out extraneous duties and fill gaps whenever and wherever the need arose. It is perhaps hardly surprising therefore that – unlike those units which could boast of pre-war histories and traditions – there was, as yet, little sense of a *Geschwader esprit* among the members of JG 52.

By the close of the French campaign the *Geschwaderstab* alone was based on the Channel coast, at le Touquet, while its three *Gruppen* were deployed across various regions of Germany on homeland defence duties.

The first part of the *Geschwader* to rejoin Major von Bernegg's *Stab* in France was III./JG 52. Departing Jever, the *Gruppe* spent nearly three weeks in and around Berlin, before staging via Holland to Coquelles – 'a mosaic of corn and potato fields to the south-west of Calais' – where it

Towards the end of the fighting in France III./JG 52 had begun applying a unique cross-hatch to the previously pristine *hellblau* finish of its *Emils* – this marking was carried over into the Battle of Britain. The quartet pictured here – all wearing inflatable life-jackets – are survivors of the *Gruppe's* disastrous ten-day participation in the Battle. The two unteroffiziere on the right, Heinrich Fullgräbe (standing) and Karl Steffen (seated on wing), are both future Knight's Cross winners who would be lost on the eastern front. The *Emil* is Steffen's 'Yellow 8', in which he claimed one of 29 July's two kills

arrived on 22 July. The *Gruppe's* stay on the Channel coast was to be of short duration. It lasted just ten days – and proved disastrous.

III./JG 52's first operation was scheduled for the early afternoon of 24 July. It was a *freie Jagd* sweep intended to help cover the withdrawal of bombers attacking a convoy in the Thames Estuary. The *Gruppe* bored in over Dover and set off northwards across Kent. All went well until the unit reached the estuary, where it was set upon by a squadron of Spitfires.

The resulting clash off Margate ended with four Bf 109s being shot down into the sea. Among the casualties was *Gruppenkommandeur* Wolf-Heinrich von Houwald and two of his *Staffelkapitäne*, Oberleutnants Herbert Fermer and Lothar Ehrlich (of 7. and 8./JG 52 respectively). To add insult to serious injury, only one of the three Spitfires claimed in return was subsequently confirmed.

Presumably on the premise that a thrown rider should immediately remount, the *Gruppe* was ordered out again 24 hours later, this time as escort to Stukas attacking a convoy in the Straits of Dover. And again they met their nemesis in the shapely form of No 610 Sqn's Spitfires. Four more Bf 109s failed to return to Coquelles. Two of those who disappeared into the Channel were Oberleutnant Willy Bielefeld, the interim *Staffelführer* of 7./JG 52, and Fermer's designated replacement Oberleutnant Wilhelm Keidel.

For a second time the *Gruppe* had but a single Spitfire to show for its pains. Future Knight's Cross recipient Unteroffizier Edmund Rossmann of 7./JG 52, who had already had two kills disallowed in recent days (a Swordfish and a Spitfire, the former during the *Gruppe's* stop-over at Leeuwarden in Holland), was again unlucky. His somewhat bizarre claim for a twin-engined French Breguet Bre 690 on this date was, perhaps not surprisingly, also rejected!

III./JG 52's unparalleled loss of its *Gruppenkommandeur* and the equivalent of four *Staffelkapitäne* in the space of little more than 24 hours (the likes of which had not befallen any other *Jagdgeschwader* to date) brought a rapid end to its cross-Channel campaigning. Two final RAF fighters claimed off Dover on 29 July were poor recompense for its own catastrophic losses. The following day the *Gruppe*, under acting-*Kommandeur* Hauptmann Wilhelm Ensslen, was withdrawn to Leeuwarden, and thence back to Zerbst to recuperate and resume its homeland defence role.

The *Geschwaderstab* at Le Touquet was not left in enforced isolation for long. The vacancy at Coquelles resulting from III. *Gruppe's* abrupt departure was filled by Hauptmann von Eschwege's I./JG 52, which flew in from Bönninghardt on 2 August. Throughout the previous month this *Gruppe* had been engaged on defence of the Reich duties under the control of JG 77.

Among the targets the *Gruppe* had protected was no less a personage than the Führer himself – not only during his major speech in Berlin's Kroll Opera House on 19 July, in which he had offered the chance of a negotiated peace to Great Britain (an offer flatly rejected by Prime Minister Winston Churchill within the hour!), but also on the occasion of his visit to the annual Richard Wagner Festival in Bayreuth four days later, when he attended a performance of his favourite composer's *Götterdämmerung*!

Members of the local home guard (Local Defence Volunteers) and police survey Leo Zaunbrecher's 'Red 14', which had belly-landed on farmland east of Lewes after clashing with a No 615 Sqn Hurricane over Hastings on 12 August. Note the bullet holes in the rear fuselage

On 6 August JG 52's strength on the Channel front was further bolstered by the arrival of II. *Gruppe* at Peuplingues, an airstrip close to Coquelles. Since late June Hauptmann von Kornatzki's II./JG 52 had been deployed along Germany's North Sea coastal belt, during which time it had been able to claim two RAF Blenheim IVs off the Friesian Islands.

Presumably mindful of III. *Gruppe's* baptism of fire on the Channel front, I./JG 52's pilots were given over a week to familiarise themselves with their new surroundings. This apparently paid off, for on their first brush with the enemy, on 11 August, they claimed four RAF machines destroyed without loss to themselves. Having had less time to acclimatise, II. *Gruppe* was credited with just one victory on this date, but received a nasty shock 24 hours later with the disappearance of three of its number. Two went into the Channel, while the third – Unteroffizier Leo Zaunbrecher's 'Red 14' – ended up on its belly with its nose among the corn stooks of a Sussex farm.

Unlike the single pilot shot down and captured during the French campaign, Zaunbrecher was the first of nearly 30 pilots of JG 52 – the

One of the RAF recovery team members was later photographed making a great play of cutting the 5. *Staffel* badge from the port side of 'Red 14's' cowling. He obviously never completed the job . . .

29

. . . as witness here the remains of 'Red 14' pictured in an aircraft dump some time later. The bullet damage in the area around the fuselage *Balkenkreuz* is even more apparent in this shot (Question: how many 'erks' does it take to lift one *Emil* wing? Answer: if there's a press photographer about, 13!)

equivalent of almost an entire *Gruppe* – to become PoWs during the course of the Battle of Britain.

Both *Gruppen* took part in *Adlertag* (Eagle Day) on 13 August. This was the 'Big Blow' intended to knock out Fighter Command's airfields in southern England, but which quickly descended into chaos and confusion due to a combination of adverse weather conditions and communications breakdowns. Eagle Day may have been inconclusive, but not so 14 August, when it cost II./JG 52 three pilots to claim a single (unconfirmed) Spitfire over Canterbury. Four days later, before it could suffer any further casualties, the *Gruppe* was transferred back up to the German Bight to resume its defence of the Reich's northern coastline.

On the day of II. *Gruppe's* departure – 18 August, the 'Hardest Day' of the entire Battle according to one eminent historian – Hauptmann Wolfgang Ewald led some half-dozen machines of his 2./JG 52 in a strafing attack on the RAF's forward fighter airfield at Manston, in Kent. Ewald's attention had been caught by a group of Spitfires bunched together on the ground preparing to refuel between sorties.

After two passes, the *Staffel* claimed the destruction of at least ten fighters, with a trio of Blenheims thrown in for good measure. In fact, just two of No 266 Sqn's Spitfires were total write-offs, with another six being severely damaged but repairable. A lone Hurricane, which had had the misfortune to land at Manston to refuel, was also destroyed.

But an event of greater importance on that 18 August was the departure of *Geschwaderkommodore* Major Hubert Merhart von Bernegg. Typical of the 'Old Guard' leadership which Göring was now intent on replacing in order to boost the poor performance (as he perceived it) of his *Jagdwaffe*, neither von Bernegg nor any of his *Stab* members – all of them of World War 1 vintage – had ever flown operationally at the head of JG 52.

The officer brought in to replace him was altogether different. Although he was himself 38 years old, Major Hanns Trübenbach – previously *Gruppenkommandeur* of I.(J)/LG 2 at nearby Calais-Marck, to which the *Stab* JG 52 now moved – was a passionate and gifted flyer. He had led the German national aerobatic team during 1938-39, and had already claimed three victories during the recent campaign in France. Determined to continue his operational career, Major Trübenbach got around the problem of having inherited a non-flying *Stab* organisation by 'borrowing' his erstwhile wingman from I.(J)/LG 2, *Gruppen*-Adjutant

Oberleutnant Ludwig Lenz, whenever he decided to fly a mission! But this would not be immediately, as a spell of cloudy, squally weather over the next five days was about to curtail both sides' activities.

26 August dawned fine and clear, however. This gave Oberleutnant Karl-Heinz Leesmann of 1./JG 52 the chance to claim his first victory – a Spitfire shot down off Margate. But it also spelt the end of the Battle for fellow *Staffel* member Feldwebel Herbert Bischoff, who was forced to land his damaged *Emil* in a field behind Westgate-on-Sea.

Forty-eight hours later another four pilots of I. *Gruppe* joined Herbert Bischoff in British captivity, and a fifth was killed, following a series of *Freie Jagd* sweeps over Kent. But, in return, I./JG 52 had succeeded in adding an equal number of RAF fighters to its own scoreboard.

That day also witnessed another command change when *Gruppenkommandeur* Hauptmann Siegfried von Eschwege left to take up a training appointment. His successor at the head of I. *Gruppe* was Hauptmann Wolfgang Ewald, whose own position as *Staffelkapitän* of 2./JG 52 was in turn filled by Oberleutnant Leesmann.

On 30 August I./JG 52 traded a Messerschmitt for a Spitfire. The latter was being flown by Leutnant Christoph Geller, the one-time *Gruppen*-Adjutant who had accompanied Hauptmann von Pfeil on his ill-fated birthday celebration flight the previous November. Now a member of 2. *Staffel*, Leutnant Geller went down into the Channel off Dover after reporting engine failure.

Another *Emil* which bellied its pilot into British captivity was 1. *Staffel's* 'White 9'. Feldwebel Herbert Bischoff forced-landed his fighter, its propeller windmilling (note the bent blades) after suffering engine failure during a dogfight over the Thames Estuary, at Westgate-on-Sea on the afternoon of 24 August

When Bischoff's Bf 109 was carted away by lorry two days later, it was snapped by a local air raid warden. This got the amateur photographer into very hot water, and he was brought before Margate Police Court charged with 'photographing the wreckage of a German aeroplane without a permit'. A serious attempt to deny intelligence to the enemy, or officialdom gone mad? A newspaper report on the incident quoted the police and military as being 'very disturbed about the large number of people who are running about with cameras taking photographs which ought not to be taken', but the magistrate adopted a more lenient view and let the culprit off with a warning. This is purportedly the photograph in question, showing a couple of New Zealand soldiers giving the warden the thumbs-up as they passed. And although the damage to the port wing looks similar – Bischoff hit a concrete anti-glider post while careering across the stubble – who straightened that propeller?

It was 2./JG 52 who also suffered 31 August's only casualty. But this date was to be the most successful of the entire Battle for I. *Gruppe*, with claims for no fewer than ten RAF fighters. Among the victors was Leutnant Hans Berthel, who added a pair of Hurricanes to the LeO 451 he had downed on 6 October 1939 to open I./JG 52's scoring.

Berthel was credited with another Hurricane the following day – one of a total of five Fighter Command aircraft destroyed over Kent. And once again it was 2. *Staffel* which sustained the sole loss when one of its aircraft came under attack south of Ashford and exploded in mid-air. On 2 September five more RAF fighters were brought down over north Kent at the cost of a single 1. *Staffel* PoW.

And so it went on. Although I./JG 52 was by now undoubtedly giving better than it got, the steady rate of attrition being suffered by the *Gruppe*, coupled with a lack of replacements, meant that by the end of the first week of September its strength in men and machines had sunk to well below 50 per cent.

On 7 September, with the Battle now approaching its climax, I./JG 52 was called upon to undertake its first bomber escort mission to London. The depleted *Gruppe's* part in this momentous major bombing raid on the enemy's capital was apparently particularly successful. Not only did it and all its assigned charges (a formation of He 111s) return without loss, four of Ewald's pilots each claimed a British fighter apiece as the huge phalanx of Luftwaffe machines – said to be more than a mile-and-a-half (2.4 km) high and covering some 800 square miles (2,070 km²) of sky – made its majestic way up-river from the mouth of the Thames Estuary.

The following day Hermann Göring, who had taken personal charge of the operation, and had stood with his entourage on the cliffs at Cap Gris

Although reminiscent of the *Sitzkrieg*, Unteroffizier Eugen Kind is not dozing away hours of boredom, but snatching a few minutes of well-deserved rest. For this is Coquelles, on the Channel Coast, in the late summer of 1940, and the Battle of Britain is at its height. Another 1. *Staffel* casualty, Eugen Kind would be killed in a dogfight over Ashford on 5 September

Nez to watch the aerial armada set out, telephoned the *Gruppe* to offer his congratulations on its performance.

Two further missions to London followed in quick succession before, early in the evening of 11 September, the action suddenly switched much nearer to home when a dozen Fairey Albacores attacked the concentration of invasion barges being assembled in Calais harbour. After an emergency scramble, 1. *Staffel* quickly downed a brace of the Fleet Air Arm biplanes, plus two of their Blenheim fighter escort.

Four days later on 15 September – now commemorated as 'Battle of Britain Day' – I./JG 52 was again en route to London, this time escorting a force of Ju 88s. Becoming embroiled in a series of savage dogfights, the *Gruppe* was able to claim eight Hurricanes (no sign of Spitfire snobbery here!) over north Kent and the Thames Estuary. Oberleutnant Karl-Heinz Leesmann's pair took his total to ten – he was the first JG 52 pilot to reach double figures. The trio credited to future fellow Knight's Cross holder Oberleutnant Helmut Bennemann meant that he was not far behind with eight. The day's only loss was Hans Berthel, who parachuted into captivity after colliding with one of the Hurricanes (a seventh 'victory' which was not credited to him!) over Staplehurst.

The next 72 hours were taken up with a number of bomber and fighter-bomber escort missions to London and Tilbury. Then, on 24 September, came I. *Gruppe's* last significant success of the Battle when it claimed (somewhat over-optimistically) seven Spitfires without loss over the Dover area.

The following day II./JG 52 flew back in to Peuplingues. During its five-week sojourn on the North Sea coast there had been two command changes. Firstly, Hauptmann Horst-Günther von Kornatzki had been appointed to the *Stab* of JFS 1 (Fighter School 1) at Werneuchen, on the outskirts of Berlin. His place as *Gruppenkommandeur* was taken by Hauptmann Wilhelm Ensslen (ex-*Staffelkapitän* of 9./JG 52). And, secondly, the confusion of the two Schumanns had finally been laid to rest with the posting of 4. *Staffel's* Oberleutnant Heinz Schumann to 2./JG 51 – the Knight's Cross-wearing Major Heinz Schumann, by then *Geschwaderkommodore* of SKG 10, would subsequently be shot down by Spitfires over Belgium in July 1943. Schumann's replacement at the head of 4./JG 52 was one Oberleutnant Johannes Steinhoff.

On 27 September the two *Gruppen* found themselves in action over Kent. I./JG 52, now reportedly just 13 aircraft strong, was credited with five enemy fighters destroyed without loss. II. *Gruppe*, which was perhaps a little rusty, fared less well. Its trio of Spitfires over Chatham cost the unit five pilots downed and captured, plus a sixth who baled out wounded into the Channel off Ramsgate.

The last day of the month saw four more pilots – two from each *Gruppe* – enter British captivity (one of them being Oberleutnant Kurt Kirchner, who had claimed I./JG 52's second kill, the reconnaissance Blenheim on 13 October 1939, and had added two Spitfires since). 30 September also witnessed the last of JG 52's bomber escort missions. Henceforth, most of the Luftwaffe's major bombing raids over Great Britain would be flown under the cover of darkness.

The onus of keeping up the pressure by day now fell upon a handful of fighter-bomber *Staffeln*. In contrast to almost every other *Jagdgeschwader*

II./JG 52 saw 11 of its pilots enter British captivity during the Battle. 4. *Staffel* was the hardest hit, with five of its members spending the rest of the war as PoWs. The unit lost two 'White 2s' within eight days of each other. The first was put down at Detling by Gefreiter Erich Mummert after suffering radiator damage during a bomber escort mission to London on 30 September. Later, it served as a handy backdrop for this souvenir snapshot of an unidentified RAF pilot

based on the Channel coast, JG 52 had never been required to convert part of its own strength for fighter-bomber operations. It had always been employed solely in fighter roles. And so it would continue. Throughout the whole of the coming month of October, JG 52's two *Gruppen* would fly almost exclusively as escorts to the Bf 109 *Jabos* of LG 2 (with an occasional *freie Jagd* or ASR sortie thrown in for good measure).

By now the Battle was rapidly winding down, as the month's figures indicate. Of the two *Gruppen*, it was the tired remnants of I./JG 52 who came off worst. Its five victories cost the unit seven more pilots – six PoWs and one missing over the Channel. Three of the former were lost on 27 October during the *Gruppe's* final mission over England. Four days later – coincidentally the official end of the Battle in British eyes – and with just four of its original 36 pilots remaining, I./JG 52 was withdrawn from operations and ordered back to Krefeld, in Germany, for rest, recuperation and re-equipment.

Although it too had been hit in the radiator (by a No 603 Sqn Spitfire over the Thames Estuary), the arrival of Feldwebel Paul Boche's 'White 2' on farmland to the east of Chelmsford on 8 October was a much less controlled affair. The *Emil* wrapped itself around a pair of particularly sturdy haystacks, with the result seen here

Krefeld was also to be the base for JG 52's newly-established *Ergänzungsstaffel*. Such *Staffeln* – literally 'supplementary squadrons' – were currently being added to every *Geschwader's* table of organisation. Their task was to prepare fully-trained pilots for frontline service, and they are perhaps best described as being each Luftwaffe unit's own 'in-house' equivalent of the RAF's more generic operational training units. Erg.St./JG 52 was officially activated on 6 October under the command of Oberleutnant Werner Lederer, ex-*Staffelkapitän* of 6./JG 52.

II. *Gruppe* would end October with eight victories for four losses – two killed and two PoW. A fifth pilot had a lucky escape when he was forced to ditch in the Channel after tangling with RAF fighters on 29 October. He was even more fortunate to be picked up by the German *Seenotdienst* (Air-Sea-Rescue service). But it was not a particularly auspicious start for Leutnant Gerhard Barkhorn, and gave little indication that he would rise to become the second most successful pilot in the *Geschwader* – and one of only two fighter pilots in history to achieve more than 300 kills!

Sadly, Gerhard Barkhorn's luck did not rub off on his *Gruppenkommandeur*, Hauptmann Wilhelm Ensslen, when he too clashed with RAF Spitfires over the Kent coast on 2 November. It is believed that Ensslen fell victim to Canadian ace Sqn Ldr J A 'Johnny' Kent, CO of No 92 Sqn. Although he managed to bale out of his machine, which crashed near Dymchurch, Hauptmann Ensslen was killed on landing. A member of his *Gruppenstab* went down into the Channel nearby, and from there into a British PoW camp.

These were JG 52's last two losses of the Battle. Three days later II. *Gruppe* was also ordered back to Germany, its destination being München-Gladbach (today's Mönchengladbach). This was only some 12 miles (20 km) to the south-west of Krefeld, where, on that same 5 November, Major Trübenbach's *Geschwaderstab* arrived to take up residence alongside I. *Gruppe* and the new *Ergänzungsstaffel*.

But it's back to I. *Gruppe* for a photograph of a pilot (and canine friend) selected to represent the many now unknown names and faces who made up the bulk of JG 52 during the early months of the war. By chance another victim of radiator damage, sustained in a clash with Spitfires during a *freie Jagd* sweep over Rochester, Oberleutnant Günther Büsgen – the acting-*Staffelkapitän* of 1./JG 52 – baled out east of Maidstone on 12 October

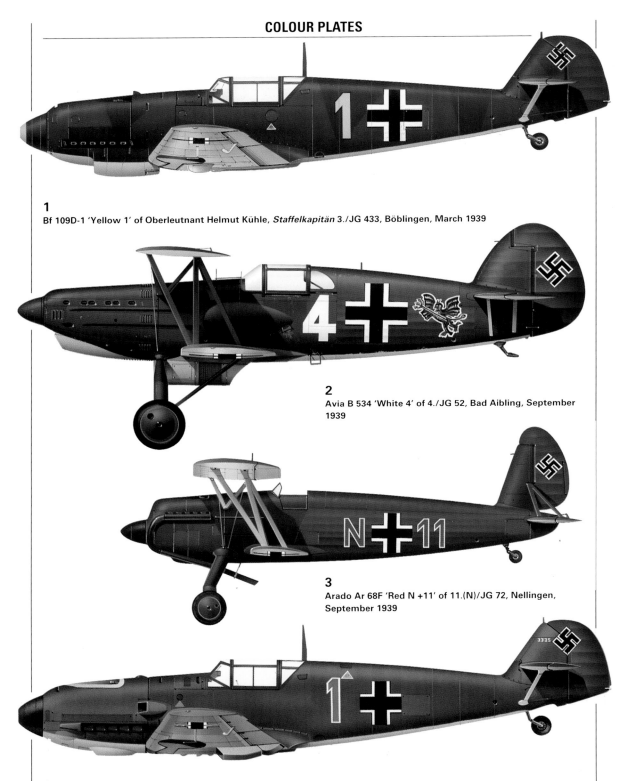

1
Bf 109D-1 'Yellow 1' of Oberleutnant Helmut Kühle, *Staffelkapitän* 3./JG 433, Böblingen, March 1939

2
Avia B 534 'White 4' of 4./JG 52, Bad Aibling, September 1939

3
Arado Ar 68F 'Red N +11' of 11.(N)/JG 72, Nellingen, September 1939

4
Bf 109E (Wk-Nr 3335) 'Red 1' of Leutnant Hans Berhel, 2./JG 52, Bonn-Hangelar, October 1939

5
Bf 109E 'Red 1' of Oberleutnant August-Wilhelm Schumann, *Staffelkapitän* 5./JG 52, Mannheim, November 1939

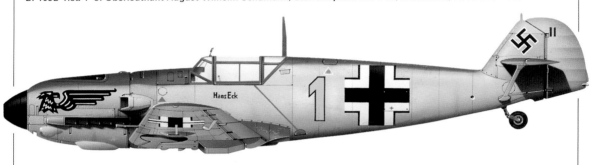

6
Bf 109E 'Yellow 1' of Oberleutnant Werner Lederer, *Staffelkapitän* 6./JG 52, Luxemborg-Sandweiler, June 1940

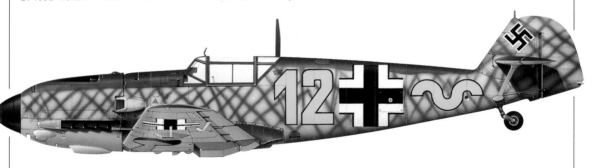

7
Bf 109E 'Yellow 12' of 9./JG 52, Hoppstädten, June 1940

8
Bf 109E 'Black Chevron and Bars' of Major Hanns Trübenbach, *Geschwaderkommodore* JG 52, Calais-Marck, September 1940

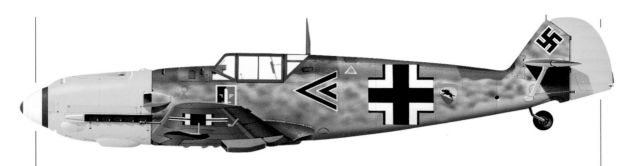

9
Bf 109E 'Black Double Chevron' of Hauptmann Wolfgang Ewald, *Gruppenkommandeur* I./JG 52, Katwijk, January 1941

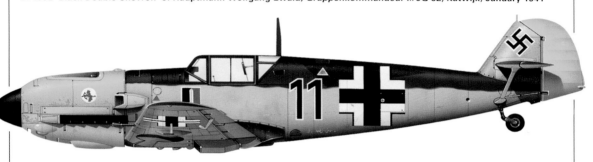

10
Bf 109E 'Black 11' of 5./JG 52, Raversidje, April 1941

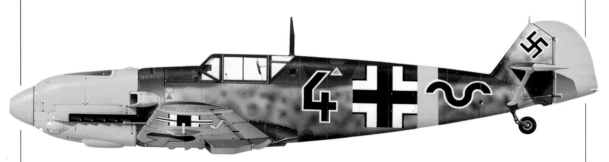

11
Bf 109E 'Black 4' of Gefreiter Friedrich Wachowiak, 8./JG 52, Bucharest-Pipera, April 1941

12
Bf 109F 'Black Chevron 4' of the *Gruppenstab* I./JG 52, Katwijk, September 1941

13
Bf 109F 'Black Chevrons and Bars' of Major Hanns Trübenbach, *Geschwaderkommodore* JG 52, Tiraspol, October 1941

14
Bf 109F 'Black 7' of 2./JG 52, Rusa, November 1941

15
Bf 109F 'Black 12' of 5./JG 52, Byelgorod, June 1942

16
Bf 19G-2 'Black Double Chevron' of Hauptmann Johannes Steinhoff, *Gruppenkommandeur* II./JG 52, Rostov, August, 1942

17
Bf 19G-2 'Yellow 5' of Leutnant Walter Krupinski, 6./JG 52, Armavir, August 1942

18
Bf 19G-2 'Black 13' of Oberleutnant Günther Rall, *Staffelkapitän* 8./JG 52, Gostanovka, August 1942

19
Bf 19G-2 'Yellow 11' of Oberleutnant Hermann Graf, *Staffelkapitän* 9./JG 52, Pitomnik, September 1942

20
Bf 109G-2/R6 'White 3' of 1./JG 52, Rostov, November 1942

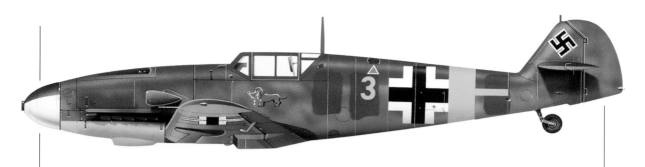

21
Bf 109G-4 'Yellow 3' of Unteroffizier Hans Waldmann, 6./JG 52, Anapa, June 1943

22
Bf 109G-4 'Black 12' of Leutnant Peter Düttmann, 5./JG 52, Anapa, July 1943

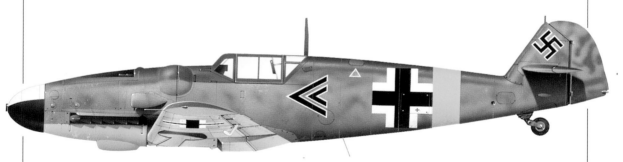

23
Bf 109G-6 'Black Double Chevron' of Hauptmann Johannes Wiese, acting-*Gruppenkommandeur* I./JG 52, Varvarovka, July 1943

24
Bf 109G-6 'Black Double Chevron' of Hauptmann Gerhard Barkhorn, *Gruppenkommandeur* II./JG 52, Poltava-North, September 1943

25
Bf 109G-6 'Black Chevron and Bars' of Oberstleutnant Dietrich Hrabak, *Geschwaderkommodore* JG 52, Kerch V, October 1943

26
Bf 109G-6 'Yellow 1' of Leutnant Erich Hartmann, *Staffelkapitän* 9./JG 52, Novo-Zaporozhe, October 1943

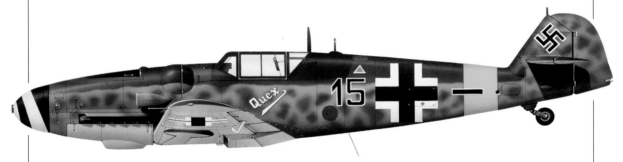

27
Bf 109G-6 'Black 15' of Leutnant Walter Wolfrum, 5./JG 52, Gramatikovo, March 1944

28
Bf 109G-6 'Yellow 3' of Leutnant Heinz Ewald, 6./JG 52, Zilistea, June 1944

29
Bf 109G-6 'White 1' of Hauptmann Erich Hartmann, *Staffelkapitän* 4./JG 52, Budaörs/Hungary, November 1944

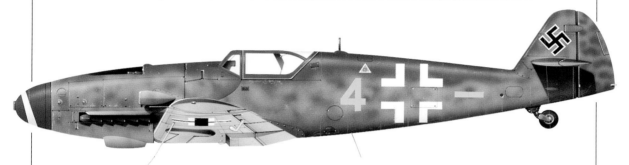

30
Bf 109G-10 'Yellow 4' of 6./JG 52, Veszprem/Hungary, February 1945

31
Bf 109G-14 'White 8' of 4./JG 52, Fels-am-Wagram/Austria, April 1945

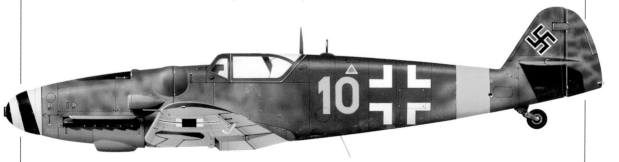

32
Bf 109G-14 'Yellow 10' of 3./JG 52, Deutsch Brod (Nemecky Brod/Czechoslovakia), May 1945

1
JG 52
worn on cowling of Bf 109E, and below windscreen of Bf 109E, F and G

2
I./JG 52 (early)
worn on cowling of Bf 109E, and on rear fuselage of Bf 109E/F

3
I./JG 52 (late)
worn on cowling of Bf 109E/F

4
2./JG 52
worn below cockpit of Bf 109G

5
3./JG 52
worn on rear fuselage of Bf 109E/F

6
4./JG 52
worn on cowling of Bf 109E, and below cockpit of Bf 109E/F

7
5./JG 52
worn on cowling of Bf 109E/F

8
6./JG 52 (early)
worn on cowling of Bf 109E

9
6./JG 52 (late)
worn below cockpit of Bf 109F

10
III./JG 52 (early)
worn on cowling of Bf 109E

11
III./JG 52 (late)
worn below windscreen of Bf 109F/G

12
7./JG 52
worn on cowling of Bf 109G

13
9./JG 52
worn below cockpit of Bf 109G

14
1./JG 71 (4./JG 52)
worn on rear fuselage of Avia B 534

15
13.(*slow.*)/JG 52
worn on cowling of Bf 109E

16
15.(*kroat.*)/JG 52
worn below windscreen of Bf 109E,
F(?) and G

17
6./JG 52
personal emblem of Unteroffizier
Hans Waldmann

18
6./JG 52
personal emblem of Leutnant Heinz
Ewald

INTERLUDE

As in the Battle of France, the *Geschwader's* performance during the recent cross-Channel campaigning had given no indication whatsoever of the greatness that was yet to come. True, between them, JG 52's pilots had claimed close on 90 enemy aircraft destroyed, but it had cost them well over half that number of their own either killed, missing or captured to do so.

In fact these figures, and this kill-to-loss ratio, compare unfavourably with – and fall well below – those of every single one of the seven other major *Jagdgeschwader* engaged in the Battle of Britain. Nor would the coming months offer any opportunities to remedy the situation. From late 1940 until the middle of 1941, Major Trübenbach's component *Gruppen* would, if anything, be even more widely scattered than at any time to date.

The first *Gruppe* to return to operations was II./JG 52. It had spent seven weeks at München-Gladbach, latterly under its new *Kommandeur*, Hauptmann Erich Woitke, ex-*Staffelkapitän* of 6./JG 3. While at Gladbach, the *Gruppe* had received several intakes of replacement pilots, some newly trained and some drafted in from other units.

Among the latter was a young fähnrich (officer cadet) who had been credited with three victories while serving on the Channel front with 1.(J)/LG 2. Unfortunately, he had also destroyed or written-off a similar number of the *Staffel's* own fighters! But it was probably his demeanour which was the main reason for his posting, for the pilot in question was a long-haired, jazz-loving young Berliner named Hans-Joachim Marseille – 'possibly the least military member of the Wehrmacht', according to one contemporary.

The antipathy between Marseille and his new *Staffelkapitän*, Oberleutnant Johannes Steinhoff of 4./JG 52, was immediate and mutual. A product of both Kriegsmarine and Luftwaffe officer training schools, Steinhoff was the very epitome of the professional military man. It is hardly surprising that he could not tolerate Marseille's Bohemian ways and disregard for petty rules, and that he lost little time in getting rid of him again. Early in 1941, Marseille found himself posted to I./JG 27. A few months later this *Gruppe* was sent to Africa, and the rest, as the saying goes, is history (see *Osprey Elite Units 12 - Jagdgeschwader 27 'Afrika'* for details).

II./JG 52 had left München-Gladbach for Holland on 22 December 1940. Its role was to defend the Dutch North Sea coast, operating first out of Leeuwarden and then from Ypenburg, on the island of Schouwen in the Scheldt Estuary.

Five days after II. *Gruppe's* arrival at Leeuwarden, I./JG 52 was also transferred to the Netherlands. Having completed re-equipment at Krefeld, it flew in to Katwijk, on the Dutch coast north of The Hague, on 27 December. The unit was charged with guarding the North Sea approaches to both Holland and northwestern Germany. The fine distinction between the *Gruppen's* responsibilities is illustrated by the fact that I./JG 52 (patrolling to seaward, and thus regarded as being 'in the

Grinning cheekily at the camera, a young Hans-Joachim Marseille poses for a snapshot during his time on the Channel front. The future 'Star of Africa' would spend less than two months with 4./JG 52 before being posted to JG 27. Who knows what the top scorer against the Western Allies might have achieved had he been allowed to stay with JG 52 and been sent up against the Red Air Force?

frontline') remained under the control of the *Geschwaderstab*, whereas II./JG 52 (responsible for protecting the coastal provinces) was subordinated to the local territorial command, *Luftgaukommando* Holland. It proved to be a lean and difficult time, however, and posed a thankless task for both in the depths of yet another harsh winter.

The only period of excitement for I./JG 52 came early in 1941 with the announcement that the *Gruppe* was to begin preparing for deployment to Sicily. But hopes of exchanging the dubious charms of the North Sea in mid-winter for the sunnier climes of the Mediterranean were dashed when the order was rescinded at the very last moment – according to the unit diary, 'just as the 20 fully-loaded Ju 52/3m transports were warming up their engines ready for take-off!'

On 10 February II. *Gruppe* left Ypenburg for Berck-sur-Mer, on the Channel coast of France, south of Le Touquet. Here, it would once again come under the command of the *Geschwaderstab*, which – having departed Krefeld on 22 January, and spent the interim at Döberitz – arrived back at Calais-Marck on 13 February.

Twenty-four hours later JG 52 celebrated its return to its old haunts by claiming a quartet of Spitfires (probably from No 66 Sqn) over Kent. One of the four fell to Major Hanns Trübenbach west of Dover. Although

A close-up of the *Geschwader* badge devised by *Kommodore* Major Hanns Trübenbach in the winter of 1940-41. Intended to instill a sense of unity among its widely scattered *Gruppen*, JG 52's 'winged sword' emblem would disappear in the eastern front security clamp-down of 1943. The pilot in the cockpit is 2. *Staffel's* Oberfeldwebel Karl Munz, whose first victory would be a Blenheim claimed off the Friesian Islands on 25 May 1941

it was his fourth personal victory, it represented the very first for the *Geschwaderstab* – after nearly 18 months of hostilities!

The following day, quite by chance, I. *Gruppe* at Katwijk was also credited with its first kills since the Battle of Britain – a Blenheim of No 114 Sqn on a reconnaissance sortie along the Dutch coast and a pair of No 615 Sqn Hurricanes engaged on a 'Rhubarb' (sweep) over Belgium.

Shortly thereafter a further round of moves took place. Leaving the defence of northeast France in the capable hands of Oberstleutnant Adolf Galland's JG 26, the *Stab* and II./JG 52 transferred in to neighbouring Belgium (the *Stab* to Maldeghem and II. *Gruppe* to five different airfields over the course of the following three months). At the same time I./JG 52 was ordered to vacate Katwijk and disperse its individual *Staffeln* on a

Half-a-dozen 'black men' and their two pilots (far left and kneeling third from right in kapok life-jacket) clown for the camera in front of a bombed-up *Emil* of II. *Gruppe* somewhere in Belgium

Further east along the coast, a larger group of I./JG 52 mechanics enjoy an impromptu guitar recital provided by the unteroffizier seated in the deckchair. Despite the Bf 109E at readiness in the background, the obviously hazy conditions have lessened the danger of an incursion by enemy bombers

succession of separate coastal airfields – some dozen in all – which would eventually encompass an arc stretching across the Dutch and German seaboards right up to Esbjerg, in Denmark. In effect, JG 52 was helping to fill the gap in northwest Europe's aerial defences between JGs 2 and 26 in France and JG 1 on the German Bight.

Of Trübenbach's two *Gruppen*, II./JG 52, based in Belgium, and therefore the nearer to England, found itself faced with two tasks. Not only were its pilots expected to continue to carry the fight to the enemy's shores (to which end 'Shorty' Schumann's 5. *Staffel* would be forced to convert to *Jabo* operations in the spring), they also had to combat RAF Fighter Command's increasingly frequent 'leans' across the Channel into northern Europe. Over the next 12 weeks the *Gruppe* would claim eight Spitfires – and a solitary Blenheim – without loss.

Meanwhile, I./JG 52, dispersed across Holland and points east, and thus well beyond the range of RAF single-engined fighters, was employed in a more purely defensive role, and would feed on an almost exclusive diet of bombers – 39 in total, and overwhelmingly Blenheims – during its time as guardians of the North Sea shores. But these successes cost the unit at least four losses in combat.

One low-level sweep over Kent by II./JG 52 in mid-April went somewhat awry. The pilots had been briefed to ground-strafe Manston airfield, but when the raiding force met bad weather the mission was scrubbed. However, one *Schwarm* of 4. *Staffel* failed to get the word, pressing on, finding the target and attacking it as ordered.

On returning to Maldeghem, or so the story goes, they were told to report to the *Gruppenkommandeur*. Hauptmann Woitke handed each a brandy and broke the news – 'JG 51 has just reported coming under attack. Nine aircraft destroyed and one man wounded in the arm'.

In fact, the errant *Schwarm*, having completely lost its bearings in the extensive cloud, had strafed II./JG 53's base at St Omer-Arques! No material damage was caused, apparently, but two pilots – one of them the *Staffelkapitän* of 4./JG 53 – and five groundcrew were slightly injured.

Cleared of deliberate sabotage, the four members of the *Schwarm* faced only minor disciplinary measures. Two would subsequently go on to win

the Knight's Cross while serving with other units – *Schwarmführer* Oberleutnant Siegfried Simsch, who would be killed in action over Norway on D-day+2 as a hauptmann and *Kommandeur* of I./JG 11, and Gefreiter Adolf Glunz (by then himself an Oberleutnant, wearing both the Knight's Cross *and* Oak leaves) who ended the war flying Me 262s with JG 7. The other two were lost during the opening weeks of *Barbarossa*.

Nine days after the St Omer incident, on 24 April, I. *Gruppe* made one of its few forays over Kent, losing Oberfeldwebel Günter Struck of 2. *Staffel*, who parachuted into captivity over Dungeness. His 'Black 6', which was shared between two pilots of No 92 Sqn – one of them Spitfire ace Sqn Ldr J E 'Jamie' Rankin – was the last JG 52 machine to crash on British soil.

It was during the latter half of April that II./JG 52 began to receive its first Bf 109Fs. *Stab* and I. *Gruppe* would start replacing their ageing *Emils* with the new F-model the following month.

On 1 May II. *Gruppe* claimed its only Blenheim of this period. Although unconfirmed, a No 105 Sqn machine did crash-land back in England after being badly shot-up by Bf 109s during an anti-shipping sortie on this date. Seven days later a pair of Spitfires downed off Deal provided firsts for two of the St Omer miscreants – future *Experte* Adolf 'Addi' Glunz and Feldwebel Georg Mayr (the latter would be killed by ground fire over Russia on 8 August).

The weather has improved along the North Sea coastal belt, but still no sign of the RAF. As the life-jacketed pilots wait near their machines, the air of expectancy is almost palpable

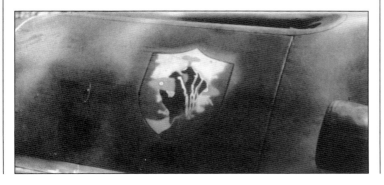

Resigning themselves to their role as guardians of the North Sea, I./JG 52 scrapped its 'running boar' badge late in the summer of 1941 for a more appropriate design featuring a black hand clutching a red Spitfire above a map of its present area of operations (as seen here adorning the cowling of one of its recently introduced *Friedrichs*). Ironically, within a few weeks the *Gruppe* would be on its way to Russia!

II./JG 52's final victories in the west were four more Spitfires shot down near Dover on 19 May. Glunz and Mayr were again credited with one apiece, the other pair both going to their *Staffelkapitän*, Oberleutnant Johannes Steinhoff. Post-war records suggest, however, that their victories were actually a trio of Hurricanes from No 306 Polish Sqn!

Meanwhile, I. *Gruppe* was taking a growing toll of Blenheims off the Dutch and German coasts – two in April and seven (plus a single Wellington) in May. The action of 15 May, which netted one of the Blenheims, also resulted in the loss of the *Gruppe's* first *Friedrich* when Leutnant Franz Bernhard's machine was hit by return fire and crashed into the sea off Texel.

Several command changes took place within the *Gruppe* at around this time. On 27 April Oberleutnant Helmut Kühle, *Staffelkapitän* of 3./JG 52, had joined the *Geschwaderstab*, his place in turn being taken by Oberleutnant Helmut Bennemann. A little under a month later, on 24 May, *Gruppenkommandeur* Hauptmann Wolfgang Ewald was posted to the staff of *Jafü* 2, whereupon 2. *Staffel's* Oberleutnant Karl-Heinz Leesmann assumed command of the *Gruppe*. Leadership of 2./JG 52 went in turn to Oberleutnant Robert Göbel.

Then, on 9 June, Hauptmann Erich Woitke's II./JG 52 suddenly received the order to retire from Belgium. Its transfer back to Münster in Germany was to be but the first leg of a journey which would take the unit eastwards into Poland in preparation for the invasion of the Soviet Union. And just four days after II. *Gruppe's* departure from Ostend-Steene, Major Trübenbach's *Geschwaderstab* was likewise pulled out of Belgium, vacating Maldeghem first for Amsterdam-Schiphol, and from there staging down into Austria.

This left just I./JG 52 guarding the North Sea coast while the world's attention became firmly focussed on the cataclysmic events now unfolding in Russia. In a vain attempt to relieve the pressure on its new-found ally in the east, the RAF stepped up its activities over northwest Europe.

This increase was reflected in I. *Gruppe's* lengthening list of kills. Thirteen Blenheims were added to its scoreboard in June, the pair claimed on the last day of the month (believed to be No 107 Sqn machines attacking Westerland) providing *Kommandeur* Oberleutnant Leesmann with victories 21 and 22.

Two Hudsons were also brought down during the month – on consecutive days – but on 10 June a 2. *Staffel* pilot had been lost in the *Gruppe's* first recorded encounter with four-engined bombers (two No 75 Sqn Stirlings sent on an abortive trip to Emden). 3./JG 52's Leutnant Hans-Reinhard Bethke balanced the account on 28 June, however, when he shot down a No 7 Sqn machine – one of six despatched against Bremerhaven – after a running battle back across the North Sea almost to within sight of the English coast, although he himself then had to be fished out of the water after failing to make it back to base.

Less easy to explain is a claim – which was confirmed! – for a B-17 destroyed just 15 minutes after Stirling N6007 went into the sea some 20 miles (32 km) off Flamborough Head. The Luftwaffe was obviously aware of the fact that the RAF had taken delivery of a small batch of Flying Fortresses, but the type's first operational mission was still ten days away.

July's five kills were all scored during the first week of the month, and consisted of three Blenheims and another Stirling/B-17 combination. The former was undoubtedly the No 7 Sqn aircraft last reported under attack from two Bf 109s northwest of Texel in the early afternoon of 1 July. The latter, claimed 30 minutes earlier, remains a mystery.

There were celebrations at the *Gruppe's* HQ on the island of Wangerooge on 23 July when it was announced that *Kommandeur* Oberleutnant Karl-Heinz Leesmann had been awarded the Knight's Cross for his 22 victories. He was the first member of JG 52 to receive the prestigious decoration, but this highlight did little to dispel the general sense of frustration being felt by his pilots.

Unable to escape the euphoric press reports and radio broadcasts issuing forth on an almost daily basis, they were only too well aware of the astronomical scores being amassed by their comrades on the eastern front. They considered the North Sea to be very much a backwater at this stage of the hostilities, and that their continued presence along its shores was both undervalued and unrewarding.

August's figures only added to their growing discontentment. It began with the loss of 3. *Staffel's* Unteroffizier Wilhelm Summerer, claimant of

Garlanded in oak leaves, Oberleutnant Karl-Heinz Leesmann celebrates 30 June's two kills – a brace of Blenheims (possibly of No 107 Sqn) brought down northwest of Texel – which took his score to 22, and won him the *Geschwader's* first Knight's Cross

the second 'B-17' almost exactly a month earlier, who was shot down by Blenheims carrying out a coastal sweep off Texel on 2 August. And after weeks of fruitless patrolling, the *Gruppe's* only successes were a trio of Blenheims destroyed north of the Friesian island of Juist on 26 August. Paradoxically, on this occasion No 82 Sqn reported that *four* of its machines had fallen victim to the enemy fighters attacking them.

But the *Gruppe's* self-styled 'exile from the real fighting' was at last approaching an end. After eight claims made in the first three weeks of September – four of them the inevitable Blenheims, the others, more surprisingly a quartet of Spitfires downed off Den Helder on the 12th – I./JG 52 was withdrawn from the North Sea area. Leaving *Stab* JG 1, under whose command it had operated for the last four months, it was now the *Gruppe's* turn to stage eastwards, rejoin its parent unit and see some action on the Russian front. And action aplenty it would indeed see, for in the next two months alone the *Gruppe* would nearly double the score it had so painstakingly amassed over the entire first two years of the war.

And, meanwhile, what of the absent III./JG 52, which had disappeared so abruptly from the Channel front after its disastrous eight days of action in the Battle of Britain?

This *Gruppe* had spent almost the whole of August 1940 at Zerbst under its new *Kommandeur*, Hauptmann Alexander von Winterfeld. Subordinated to *Luftgaukommando III* (Berlin), its role was ostensibly to protect the Junkers aircraft works at nearby Dessau. In reality, the time at

Assuming command of III./JG 52 immediately after its disastrous participation in the Battle of Britain, Hauptmann Alexander von Winterfeld sought to boost morale with the introduction of a *Gruppe* badge. The design was based on the 'Winterfeld wolf', which was taken from his family's coat-of-arms. These two NCO pilots appear singularly unimpressed by the innovation

After transferring to Rumania, the *Gruppe's* oval badge quickly disappeared beneath a coat of fresh yellow paint, as every *Emil* was given a full set of Balkan theatre markings. Some who made the trip to the south-east would not be coming back . . .

Zerbst was more of a breathing space to allow III./JG 52's pilots to recuperate from their recent mauling.

On 30 August the *Gruppe* moved closer to Berlin, first to Neuruppin, and then to Schönwalde, where it was better placed to defend the nation's capital. By now, however (well before the Battle of Britain had run its course), Hitler was already laying his plans for the invasion of the Soviet Union the following year. As part of his preparations, he was anxious to increase his presence, and extend his influence, in south-eastern Europe. This would not only provide a jumping-off point for the assault on southern Russia, it would also safeguard the region's oilfields against possible air attack from British forces in the eastern Mediterranean.

His path was eased by fellow dictator Marshal Ion Antonescu of Rumania, who had forced King Carol II to abdicate on 6 September and taken over in his stead. Antonescu, who would lead his country into joining the Axis Tri-Partite Pact on 23 November 1940, needed little persuasion to allow a *Deutsche Militärmission in Rumänien* to be established on Rumanian soil.

III./JG 52 was to provide part of the aerial component of the Mission. At first, only the *Gruppenstab*, now led by Major Gotthard Handrick

. . . 'Black 9' for example, seen in the illustration above, appears to be an almost certain candidate for the scrapyard after suffering severe damage in a taxiing accident at Bucharest-Pipera

(ex-*Kommandeur* of JG 26) and a reinforced 9. *Staffel* were involved. They left Schönwalde on 12 October and, staging via Liegnitz in Lower Silesia, arrived at Bucharest-Pipera 48 hours later. One minor oddity is the fact that on the day they departed Schönwalde, Major Handrick's *Stab* was redesignated I./JG 28 (with 9./JG 52 becoming 3./JG 28 accordingly). And when 7. and 8./JG 52 flew to Bucharest, via Vienna, to join them late in November, they in turn became 1. and 2./JG 28 respectively.

A brand new III./JG 52 was then to have been activated back in Germany, but second thoughts must have prevailed, for the order was

With a clutch of Rumanian civil airliners in the left background, this impeccable line-up of III./JG 52's Bf 109Es must have impressed Germany's new ally mightily . . .

. . . despite the fact that there was initially very little for the *Gruppe* to do in Rumania. This photograph captures the dearth of activity perfectly – a bored Feldwebel plays with his new-found furry friend while 'White 14' waits patiently beside him, starting-handle in place, but with nowhere to go

Although force of circumstances meant that III./JG 52 did not score a single kill from July 1940 to June 1941, Oberleutnant Günther Rall remains the archetypal Luftwaffe fighter pilot – complete with sunglasses and polka-dot silk scarf – as he addresses the men of his 8. *Staffel* at Bucharest-Pipera in the spring of 1941

The Cretan campaign was the swan-song of the Bf 109E in frontline service with JG 52 (although it would continue to soldier on with the *Ergänzungs* units). In the second week of June 1941 the *Emils* of III. *Gruppe*, like 'White 6' pictured here, returned to Bucharest to be replaced by Bf 109F-4s in preparation for the invasion of the Soviet Union

quickly countermanded and Major Handrick's I./JG 28, together with his three *Staffeln*, all resumed their original identities again as of 4 January 1941.

Bucharest-Pipera was to be the *Gruppe's* base for more than seven months, which passed in almost total tranquility, making I. *Gruppe's* 'North Sea backwater' seem positively action-packed by comparison. The feared RAF raids on the area's oilfields failed to materialise, and Major Handrick's pilots spent a lot of their time helping their Rumanian counterparts familiarise themselves with their newly-delivered Bf 109Es.

Not even the launch of Operation *Marita*, the invasion of neighbouring Yugoslavia on 6 April 1941, could shatter the calm. Held back in reserve – the Führer was still concerned about the vulnerability of Rumania's oil installations – the only contribution that III./JG 52 made to the campaign was to relinquish some of its *Emils* to make good the losses suffered by other *Jagdgruppen* more directly involved in the fighting.

Then, on 25 May, III./JG 52 was suddenly ordered down to Molaoi, an airfield near the southern tip of the Greek Peloponnese peninsula. Yugoslavia and Greece had by this time both surrendered, and the battle for the island of Crete, invaded by Luftwaffe airborne forces on 20 May, was at its height. Molaoi currently housed JG 77, which was heavily engaged over and around the island, and it was to this *Jagdgeschwader* that Major Handrick's *Gruppe* was subordinated to provide necessary, and welcome, reinforcement. For nearly three weeks – mainly out of Molaoi, but with some detachments later operating from Maleme airstrip, on the island itself – III./JG 52 played a small part in the subjugation of Crete.

Facing little or no aerial opposition, the *Gruppe* was initially employed primarily in ground-strafing those enemy troops still holding out on the island. Later they flew anti-shipping sorties against the vessels attempting to evacuate the defenders by sea to Egypt. III./JG 52 suffered no combat losses during these operations, but some half-dozen *Emils* were written-off, mainly in crash-landings at either Molaoi or Maleme, and two pilots were injured.

On 10 June, ten days after Crete was finally secured, the *Gruppe* returned, via Tatoi, to Bucharest-Pipera. Here, in the space of little more than a week, pilots completed their conversion on to the Bf 109F. The reason for the haste was soon apparent. Within hours the first German troops were crossing the Soviet Border.

EASTERN FRONT – ADVANCE

Operation *Barbarossa* – Hitler's long-planned invasion of the Soviet Union, finally launched in the early hours of 22 June 1941 – was to lift the curtain on the last two acts in the history of JG 52.

It heralded the emergence of the *Geschwader* from its position of very nearly second-rate nonentity – a 'filler-in-of-gaps' for other units – to one of equality with, and ultimately supremacy over, every other *Jagdgeschwader* in Göring's Luftwaffe. Individual pilots' scores would no longer be laboriously accumulated one or two at a time. Many would quickly climb into the dozens and beyond. Those of the more skilled (or simply more fortunate) *Experten* would be counted in triple figures, and the only two fighter pilots in the world to top the 300-victory mark would both be members of JG 52. Each *Gruppe's* collective score would rise into the thousands, and the *Geschwader's* final overall total – which had numbered less than 200 before *Barbarossa* – would surpass a staggering, and unprecedented, 10,000 enemy aircraft destroyed.

An indication of the official recognition accorded to JG 52 during its service on the eastern front is provided by the number of awards conferred upon its pilots. In contrast to Karl-Heinz Leesmann's solitary 'western'

Like every other *Blitzkrieg* campaign before it, *Barbarossa* began with the Luftwaffe attempting to destroy the enemy's air force on the ground. The exact date and location of this photograph, which shows the wreckage of four Tupolev SB-2 light bombers and a single Polikarpov fighter, are not known. But from the marks left by the machines, it would appear that attempts had been made to save them either by taxiing or dragging them into the shelter of the trees beyond the perimeter track

Knight's Cross, no fewer than 54 such decorations would be awarded to the *Geschwader* in the east! In addition, 14 members of JG 52 would be further honoured with the Oak Leaves, six with Swords and two with Diamonds.

And the stage upon which all these successes would be achieved was quite unlike anything the *Geschwader* had experienced before. The air war on the eastern front was predominantly tactical. Weather permitting, it was one of constant movement. But not movement in the sense of major re-deployments from one area or theatre to another, such as JG 52 had been subjected to in the past. The war in the east was dictated by the manoeuvring of the ground armies. Air units either followed in their wake as they advanced, or retired ahead of them as they retreated. Consequently, moves were frequent, and often over short distances.

JG 52's component *Gruppen* and *Staffeln* transferred base some 400 times while fighting the Soviets. Many pilots' log-books list up to 50 or more separate moves in less than two years.

Given the sheer weight of numbers involved, it is no longer possible to itemise and analyse individual kills. Nor is it feasible to detail the numerous moves made and bases occupied, some for only a matter of hours. In fact, many of these 'bases' were nothing more than large fields, or open stretches of steppe – arbitrarily selected, and just as summarily abandoned – which, during their brief span of existence, were known by the name of the nearest village, hamlet or collective farm.

True to past form, however, the opening rounds of *Barbarossa* found JG 52 in its usual fragmented state. Major Trübenbach's *Geschwaderstab* was in Vienna en route to join III. *Gruppe* as part of the *Deutsche Luftwaffen-Mission Rumänien*. The re-titled Mission was now itself a component of *Luftflotte* 4, the air command in overall control of the southern sector of the Russian front.

II./JG 52, in contrast, had been attached to JG 27, which was tasked with providing fighter cover for the close support units of General von Richthofen's VIII. *Fliegerkorps* operating under *Luftflotte* 2 on the central sector. And I./JG 52 was, of course, still stolidly guarding the North Sea coast!

Hauptmann Erich Woitke's II./JG 52 spent the opening rounds of *Barbarossa* on the central sector under the command of *Stab* JG 27. By the second week of July the unit were sharing a crowded Lepel – 80 miles (130 km) northeast of Minsk – with two other *Gruppen*. In the right foreground is 5. *Staffel's* 'Black 3'

Hauptmann Erich Woitke's II. *Gruppe* enjoyed the greater success on the first day of the campaign. Dispersed at Suwalki and Sobolevo (neighbouring airfields close to the one-time Polish frontier with Lithuania), II./JG 52 participated in the opening hours' surprise attacks on Soviet airfields and other military installations just across the border. Compared to some other units, however, the *Gruppe's* mixed bag of 16 Soviet bombers and fighters shot down was relatively modest. It is estimated that some 320+ Red Air Force machines fell victim to German fighters and flak on 22 June 1941.

But nearly five times that number of enemy aircraft – some 1500 in all – were claimed destroyed on the ground. At least one source suggests that II./JG 52 was directly involved in these operations too, with several *Schwärme* having been trained for the *Jabo* role and now flying Bf 109s fitted with large ventral panniers, each carrying 96 small SD-2 fragmentation bombs. These devilish little devices, weighing only 4.4 lbs (2 kg) each, were highly effective, but posed almost as great a danger to the pilots delivering them as to those on the receiving end (see *Osprey Aircraft of the Aces 37 - Bf 109 Aces of the Russian Front* for further details).

So astronomical were the claims being made that at first even the Luftwaffe's own High Command, including Commander-in-Chief Hermann Göring, refused to believe them. It was only when the 31 main Soviet air bases that had been the day's targets had been overrun, and investigations could be carried out on the ground, that the extent of the destruction was not only proven, but found to be even greater than estimated.

This evidence was not long in forthcoming, for once the Russians' border defences had been breached, armoured spearheads began to surge forwards along the entire length of the front. Subordinated to JG 27, Hauptmann Woitke's II./JG 52 was charged with securing the airspace above the divisions of *Panzergruppe* 3 as they advanced through Lithuania and prepared to encircle Minsk from the north. The capital of White Russia, Minsk lay at the western end of the 400-mile (640 km) Moscow highway. Its capture would be the first stepping stone towards the ultimate objective – the enemy's capital.

Minsk was the first great 'cauldron' battle of the eastern front. It lasted just 12 days, from encirclement on 27 June until final reduction on 9 July, and resulted in the capture of nearly one-third of a million Soviet troops (only some 15,000 less than the entire Allied force evacuated from Dunkirk).

II./JG 52's successes in the air above the 'cauldron' – especially over Borrisov, to the east – were no less spectacular. In one 48-hour period alone on 2-3 July, its pilots claimed 36 enemy aircraft destroyed. Exactly three-quarters of that number were Ilyushin DB-3 bombers attempting to smash an escape route through the ring of armour around Minsk. Five fell to the *Staffelkapitän* of 4./JG 52, Oberleutnant Johannes Steinhoff, and two others provided long-awaited firsts for a pair of future Knight's Cross holders, Unteroffizier Willi Nemitz and Leutnant Gerhard Barkhorn.

At 30 years of age, *'Altvater'* ('Old Father') Nemitz was one of the Luftwaffe's oldest operational fighter pilots. Having joined II. *Gruppe* on the Channel coast the previous year, he would amass 81 kills before he was himself shot down over the Caucasus in April 1943. It had taken Gerhard

Unlike 'Black 3', seen on page 58, the cowling of 4./JG 52's 'White 10' has been given a thin wash of yellow paint. Although care has been taken not to obscure the *Staffel's* small 'black cat' badge forward of the supercharger air intake, it is almost hidden here by the propeller blade

Barkhorn 120 missions – and an involuntary dip in the Channel – to achieve his first victory. Another 300 were to follow before war's end!

For the rest of July II./JG 52 would accompany the rampaging Panzers across Lithuania and into Russia proper as they drove hard for Smolensk. This was the next major town on the Moscow highway, situated almost exactly mid-way along its length, and soon to be the scene of another great 'cauldron' battle. Flying both Stuka- and bomber-escort sorties, as well as *freie Jagd* sweeps, Hauptmann Woitke's pilots added close on another 70 kills to their overall total.

Then, on 5 August – the very day that the last troops of the three Soviet armies trapped in the Smolensk pocket surrendered – II./JG 52 suddenly received orders to move. Leaving its base outside Vitebsk, to the northwest of the 'cauldron', the *Gruppe* (together with elements of JG 27) transferred 200 miles (320 km) northwards to Solzy. Here, close to Lake Ilmen, it came under the command of the northern sector's *Luftflotte* 1.

In the southern sector, III./JG 52's new Bf 109F-4s retained the large numerals (and wavy bar) carried by the unit's earlier *Emils*. But the *Gruppe's* 'running wolf' badge had not long survived the departure of Hauptmann Alexander von Winterfeld. Under *Kommandeur* Major Albert Blumensaat the unit's *Friedrichs* now sported a different emblem – a barbed red cross – below the windscreen on either side of the fuselage. Note the pilot's life-jacket, worn for overwater patrols along the Black Sea coast

Oberleutnant Günther Rall, the *Staffelkapitän* of 8./JG 52, scored his first eastern front kill – an Ilyushin DB-3 near Constanza – 48 hours into the campaign

And it was along this northernmost stretch of the front, from Lake Ilmen up to Leningrad, on the Baltic, that the unit would operate throughout August and September.

But while II./JG 52 had been covering the advance of *Panzergruppe* 3's seven divisions more than halfway to Moscow (and taking in two great 'cauldron' battles on the way), what of III./JG 52's activities on the southern sector?

On the eve of *Barbarossa*, the *Gruppenstab* and 8. and 9. *Staffeln* had all vacated Bucharest for Mizil, an airfield 40 miles (64 km) north of the Rumanian capital, and close to the oilfields of Ploesti. Hitler was still concerned about protecting these vital installations, and now with good reason. Once hostilities with the Soviet Union commenced, the Red Air Force would pose a much greater, more tangible and infinitely closer threat – the Russian border was less than 46 miles (75 km) away – than a few hard-pressed RAF squadrons already fully engaged against the Axis in the far-off Mediterranean.

In the event, Soviet bombers seemed reluctant to venture even this short diatance into enemy airspace. Although the Ploesti complex would be attacked on later occasions, the Russians at first confined their activities to bombing targets along Rumania's Black Sea coastline, including the country's major seaport and oil terminal at Constanza. III./JG 52 thus found itself with very little to do during the first 48 hours of its eastern front war.

It was 24 June before the unit was successfully vectored down to the coast to intercept several formations of Ilyushin bombers over the Constanza area .The unescorted DB-3s proved easy prey, and the *Gruppe* claimed a round dozen of their number. One of them provided Oberleutnant Günther Rall, now *Staffelkapitän* of 8./JG 52, with his second kill – he added a Tupolev SB-2 the following day. But it was on 26 June, when the Russians attempted to launch a combined naval and air bombardment against Constanza, that the *Gruppe* achieved its biggest success of its entire time in Rumania. The assault cost the Soviet Black Sea Fleet the destroyer flotilla leader *Moskva*, and the Red Air Force lost another 18 unescorted bombers, all downed by pilots of III./JG 52.

After these three hectic days over and around Constanza, which had seen 35 enemy bombers destroyed for the loss of a single *Friedrich*, the following week was to prove entirely barren. Not a single claim was made, despite the three *Staffeln* being rotated in turn down to Mamaia, an airfield on the coast just north of Constanza. It nevertheless came as something of a shock when, on 4 July, the *Gruppe* received a telegram from their Commander-in-Chief. Addressed to their new *Kommandeur*, Major Albert Blumensaat, it read, in effect;

'Your unit continues to distinguish itself by its failure to shoot down the enemy. Just how much longer are the Russians to be allowed to enter your airspace unmolested?

'Signed: Göring'

This petulant missive clearly revealed just how out of touch the Reichsmarschall was. Bedazzled by the huge scores being racked up in the skies above the titanic land battles currently raging in the central sector, he now accepted these as the norm. Anything less came close to being regarded as dereliction of duty. Protest was pointless, as too was any attempt to explain the completely different conditions to be found along the Rumanian coastal belt, where hit-and-run raiders – approaching undetected over the open waters of the Black Sea – could still strike almost at will at any point along more than 200 miles (320 km) of shoreline, and quickly disappear back out to sea again.

A scapegoat had to be found. For some reason the axe fell upon Hauptmann Erwin Bacsilla, *Staffelkapitän* of 7./JG 52 which, throughout much of this period, had been kept back at Bucharest-Pipera. He was relieved of his command on 11 July.

But Göring's telegram did contain a grain of truth. Although a pair of (unconfirmed) DB-3s had been claimed on the day it was sent, the remainder of July saw just 12 more enemy aircraft added to III./JG 52's scoreboard – and three of these were antiquated single-engined reconnaissance flying boats of the Soviet Navy. It was not until 1 August, when the *Gruppe* was transferred inland to Belaya-Zerkov, south of the Ukrainian capital Kiev, that its fortunes changed.

In the first week of August, operating under the temporary control of JG 3, Major Blumensaat's pilots were credited with 38 enemy aircraft destroyed. This number, of which all but five were fighters, took the Gruppe's collective total beyond the one hundred figure (a milestone passed by II./JG 52 over five weeks earlier).

Two of 4 August's 20 kills were firsts for another pair of leading personalities in the story of JG 52. Escorting a formation of Ju 87 Stukas southeast of Kiev on that date, 9. *Staffel's* Leutnant Hermann Graf brought down an I-16 *Rata*. His wingman, Unteroffizier Leopold

If his choice of headgear is anything to go by, this unknown 7. *Staffel* pilot is finding the Rumanian summer sun a little too much to bear! Unfortunately, the five victory bars on the rudder (each decorated with a red star) do little to help his identification – some half-dozen members of 7./JG 52 had been credited with five or more Soviet machines before August was out

Steinbatz, claimed another of the rotund Polikarpovs five minutes later. Hermann Graf was to end the war not only as *Kommodore* of JG 52, but also as one of only two members of the *Geschwader* to be awarded the Diamonds. 'Bazi' Steinbatz would not survive the conflict.

The successes of early August set the pattern for the immediate weeks to come, firstly in the fighting around Kiev and then, from the middle of the month onwards, further to the southeast along the line of the lower Dnieper. German troops had managed to gain several footholds across this natural barrier, which flowed through Kiev down to the Black Sea. The Soviet Air Force reacted furiously, sending in waves of bombers in an attempt to contain these bridgeheads on the eastern bank of the Dnieper and prevent the Germans from breaking out into the open steppe beyond (a scenario reminiscent of the previous year's Anglo-French attacks on the Meuse crossings).

Despite the unseasonably early onset of a spell of wet and foggy weather at the beginning of September, the *Gruppe* spent the best part of a month defending the Dnieper bridgeheads. It was over the largest of them, at Dnepropetrovsk, that the unlucky successor to Hauptmann Bacsilla at the head of 7. *Staffel*, Oberleutnant Hans-Jörg Zimmermann, was killed on 1 September when he collided with his wingman during a low-level strafing run.

On 12 September III./JG 52 was transferred lower down the Dnieper to Berislav. From here it was intended to support the spearheads of 11. *Armee* as they advanced across the Perekop isthmus down into the Crimea. But the unit had been at Berislav for only three days when it was suddenly ordered to stage back to Belaya Zerkov, where the battle for Kiev was nearing its end. This second stay at Belaya was to last less than a week, for on 24 September – two days before 6. *Armee* finally reduced the huge Kiev 'cauldron', taking some 665,000 prisoners and virtually wiping out the Soviets' South-Western Front armies in the process – III./JG 52 was moved forward 200 miles (320 km) almost due east to Poltava.

While 6. *Armee* had been investing the Kiev pocket, other units had kept up the inexorable, and seemingly unstoppable, advance. Elements of 17. *Armee* were already closing in on Kharkov.

September brought an end to the good weather, with the early onset of rain. 8. *Staffel's* 'Black 6', sitting on a muddy airstrip somewhere along the Dnieper front with its cowling open (note supercharger air intake just visible above the cockpit roof), is obviously the cause of some concern to the knot of mechanics clustered around its port wing

For the next four weeks III./JG 52's activities would centre around this great industrial city, and its three major Soviet airfields. Subordinated directly to IV. *Fliegerkorps*, the *Gruppe* flew its usual mix of escort and *freie Jagd* missions. Individual and collective scores began to escalate, with pilots of the calibre of Graf and Rall adding regularly to their scores. But it was the little-known Feldwebel Gerhard Köppen of Rall's 8. *Staffel* who was leading the field with 31 victories to his credit by the time III./JG 52 departed Poltava on 23 October.

While the *Gruppe* had been shuttling backwards and forwards across the southern sector in support of all three of that area's component land *Armeen* in turn, II./JG 52 had been leading a far more sedentary existence along the Leningrad-Lake Ilmen front in the north. But lack of mobility did not mean lack of incident. Hauptmann Woitke's pilots were still ahead in the scoring stakes, and continuing to add to their lengthening list of victories. In one three-day period towards the end of August they claimed 30 Soviet aircraft destroyed.

Six of that number had fallen to the guns of Oberleutnant Johannes Steinhoff, *Staffelkapitän* of 4./JG 52. One more kill (an I-15 downed on

Seen here at a later date, wearing the sleeve patch of a Hauptmann, 4./JG 52's then Oberleutnant Johannes Steinhoff was awarded the *Geschwader's* first eastern front Knight's Cross on 30 August for a total of 35 aircraft destroyed (the first eight of which had been claimed in the west)

29 August) took 'Mäcki' Steinhoff's total to 35, and earned him the *Geschwader's* first eastern front Knight's Cross the following day.

Success came at a price, however. During its time on the northern sector II. *Gruppe* would lose two more links with its early history. On 11 August Oberfeldwebel Georg Mayr's 'White 5' was brought down by ground fire while engaged in low-level strafing. Mayr had been one of the wingmen in the *Schwarm* which had mistakenly attacked II./JG 53 at St Omer. And on 6 September Oberleutnant August-Wilhelm Schumann was killed. 'Shorty' Schumann had just claimed his 16th victory, and was indulging in a beat-up of the *Gruppe's* base at Lyuban, 52 miles (85 km) southeast of Leningrad, when his wing clipped an obstruction and he went in. His place as *Staffelkapitän* of 5./JG 52 was taken by Oberleutnant Siegfried Simsch (incidentally, another member of the 'St Omer *Schwarm*').

But it was in terms of aircraft that the *Gruppe* suffered the greater attrition. The northern sector had also been experiencing its fair share of early autumnal rain, mud and fog, and a number of Bf 109s were written off or damaged in weather-related accidents. And when II./JG 52 was ordered back down to the central sector at the end of September, it had barely a dozen serviceable machines on strength.

The reason for the *Gruppe's* recall was the imminent launch of one final all-out push to capture Moscow. Army Group Centre's Operation *Taifun* (Typhoon) was an ambitious undertaking, comprising no fewer than 14 armoured, 8 mechanised and 56 infantry divisions.

A major redeployment of Luftwaffe units was required to support this concentration of ground strength. And Hauptmann Woitke's II. *Gruppe* was not the only part of JG 52 to be involved in the central sector build-up. The needs of *Taifun* also brought an end – at long last – to I. *Gruppe's* nine-month guardianship of the North Sea coast.

Having departed the Netherlands on 24 September, Oberleutnant Karl-Heinz Leesmann's I./JG 52 reached the eastern front on 2 October, claiming a solitary I-16 on the very afternoon of its arrival. 2 October also marked the official launch of Operation *Taifun*, with Army Group Centre's divisions jumping off from their positions east of Smolensk for the last-lap, 165-mile (270 km) thrust to the Soviet capital.

Both I. and II. *Gruppen* supported the opening phases of the offensive, operating under the temporary command of JG 27. Then, on 20 October,

Arriving at Bucharest five days into *Barbarossa*, the *Geschwaderstab* spent the best part of the next three months in Rumania. Here, the *Kommodore's* F-4 kicks up a trail of late summer dust as it taxies out for a sortie. The location is possibly Mamaia, on the Rumanian Black Sea coast north of Constanza, which the *Stab* used as a forward landing ground throughout the time it was based at Bucharest-Pipera

Major Hanns Trübenbach prepares to board the same *Friedrich* (Wk-Nr 7087) seen on page 65. A long leather greatcoat may seem an unusual choice of flying gear, but Trübenbach was not off on yet another patrol. This photograph, taken at Tiraspol on 10 October 1941, records his departure for Fürth-Buchschwabach, where he was to assume command of JFS 4 (Fighter School 4) five days later. Since taking over the *Geschwader* at the height of the Battle of Britain, the 39-year-old Hanns Trübenbach had claimed five kills

Stab JG 52 flew up from the southern sector. Under new *Kommodore* Major Wilhelm Lessmann, the *Stab* took up residence alongside II. *Gruppe* at Kalinin South-West, where it was also soon joined by I./JG 52. It was at this juncture that Major Lessmann inherited a *Staffel* of Spanish volunteers – 5.(*span.*)/JG 27 – from the departing JG 27 (see *Osprey Aviation Elite Units 12 - Jagdgeschwader 27 'Afrika'* for further details).

By now Russian resistance in front of Moscow was stiffening, and the move up to Kalinin, little more than 105 miles (170 km) northwest of the capital, was perhaps a 'base too far'. Kalinin was close behind the front lines, and Lessmann's pilots found themselves within range of enemy artillery fire. The bombardment became so severe that they were soon forced to retire to another airfield in the Kalinin complex slightly further to the rear. But this brought little respite. If anything, the situation grew worse, with the groundcrews having to take up arms to defend the base against the encroaching enemy. And on 30 October, after II. *Gruppe's* dispersal area was hit by a salvo of shells which destroyed or damaged eight of the its *Friedrichs*, JG 52 was pulled back further still.

Taifun, which had started off so well, with two more successful 'cauldron' battles – at Vyazma and Bryansk – was now beginning to run into real difficulties. The Red Army was not the only enemy hindering the German advance. As October's rains gave way to snow and frost, Army Group Centre was faced with that most implacable of all opponents encountered by every foreign invader of Russian soil – 'General Winter'.

Having moved forward again, *Stab*, I. and II./JG 52 would spend most of November at Rusa, an airfield to the north of the Moscow highway. They were now only some 57 miles (92 km) short of the Soviet capital. Weather conditions permitting, they doggedly continued to fly Stuka-

escort and *freie Jagd* missions as troop movements ground slowly to a halt beneath them. By 2 December – the day Oberleutnant Johannes Steinhoff became the first member of the *Geschwader* to achieve 50 kills – Army Group Centre's strength was all but exhausted.

On 6 December, using fresh troops brought in from Siberia, the Red Army launched the first phase of a major counter-offensive along the Kalinin front to the north of Moscow. Ten days later a second attack followed on the Bryansk front to the south of the capital. Now themselves in danger of being encircled by this vast pincer movement, the divisions of Army Group Centre – ill-prepared and ill-equipped for the worsening weather – had no option but to undertake a risky and costly withdrawal out of the incipient Russian 'cauldron', before digging in for the winter. The threat to Stalin's capital had been lifted. *Barbarossa* had failed.

JG 52 had been caught up in the general retreat, and both *Gruppen* were forced to retire to Dugino, south of Vyazma. I./JG 52 had to abandon much of its technical equipment in the process, while ground crews of II. *Gruppe* sustained heavy casualties in firefights with the Soviet troops snapping at their heels. Both *Gruppen* were to spend the depths of the winter at Dugino, suffering in temperatures of -40 degrees or more, before being rotated in turn back to Jesau, in East Prussia, for rest and re-equipment early in 1942.

While German forces in the central sector – including the bulk of JG 52 – had been denied the prize of Moscow by a combination of stubborn enemy resistance and sub-zero temperatures, III. *Gruppe* had been having a slightl easier time in the far south. Here, the weather conditions were not quite so arctic, and the Red Army was still slowly giving ground.

With *Gruppenkommandeur* Major Blumensaat posted away to a training school, and his official replacement not yet arrived, III. *Gruppe*

Standing on a snow-covered apron in front of a sizeable (and intact!) hangar, 5./JG 52's winter-camouflaged 'Black 6' poses for a commemorative photograph with the *Staffel's* collective scoreboard. The number of Soviet kills recorded here (73) would place it as early December 1941 (the unit's 73rd was reportedly a U-2 downed by *Staffelkapitän* Oberleutnant Siegfried Simsch on 30 November), but this was at the height of the final push on Moscow. Would there have been time for souvenir snapshots at such a critical stage of the campaign – or was this picture taken later, perhaps even back at Jesau, in January 1942?

was under the temporary command of Hauptmann Franz Hörnig, the *Staffelkapitän* of 9./JG 52, when it departed Poltava and headed back down to the Perekop isthmus on 23 October.

The leading elements of 11. *Armee* were finally on the point of breaking through the strong Russian defences across the neck of the isthmus and gaining a foothold on the Crimean peninsula itself. The German troops were being subjected to constant air attack, however, and it was the job of III. *Gruppe*, operating under the control of JG 77, to protect them from this harassment as they began to fan southwards across the Crimea.

Hauptmann Hörnig's pilots found rich pickings among the Soviet fighters and light bombers ground-strafing the 11. *Armee* spearheads. On 24 October alone they were credited with 18 aircraft destroyed. But, in keeping with their role as the southern sector's 'fire brigade' unit, it was not long before III./JG 52 was on the move again. After just ten days over the Crimea, and with another 60+ kills added to its overall total, the *Gruppe* was transferred eastwards to Taganrog, on the shores of the Sea of Azov, on 2 November.

The unit's new base was little more than 40 miles (64 km) from Rostov-on-Don, which had been captured by 1. *Panzerarmee* on that very day. An important railway junction and industrial centre, Rostov sat astride the main route down into the oil-rich Caucasus region. The Red Army immediately launched a desperate series of counter-attacks in an attempt to wrest the city back from the Germans. For the next five weeks III./JG 52's operations would be centered over and around the North Caucasian capital. And they would be aided in their endeavours by a newly attached *Staffel* of Croatian volunteers, 15.(*kroat.*)/JG 52 (see Osprey *Aircraft of the Aces 49 - Croatian Aces of World War 2* for further details).

The 18 victories of 24 October, taking III. *Gruppe* to a total of 341, meant that it had just overtaken nearest rival II./JG 52, whose overall tally stood at 336 as of that date – having missed the high-scoring opening rounds of *Barbarossa*, I. *Gruppe* was perforce still a long way behind with only 148 kills. The fierce fighting around Rostov saw III./JG 52's lead increase dramatically as its pilots now surged towards the 500 mark.

Much more typical of the Luftwaffe's plight in the harsh winter of 1941-42 is this shot of 6./JG 52's 'Yellow 5' – possibly the mount of future *Experte* Leutnant Walter Krupinski – seen abandoned on the edge of a central sector field and now almost covered by drifting snow. Just visible is 6. *Staffel's* short-lived 'coiled cobra' emblem on a small disc below the cockpit

Their most successful day occurred exactly one week after their arrival at Taganrog, when they downed 20 Soviet aircraft. Then, on 23 November, they encountered and claimed their first examples of a new and formidable opponent. Ilyushin's heavily-armoured Il-2 *Sturmovik* ground-assault aircraft – over 36,000 of which were to be built – was to emerge as perhaps the most potent symbol of the Red Air Force's cataclysmic struggle against the invading Wehrmacht. But the machine had yet to gain its reputation of near invincibility, and in one five-minute engagement to the south of Rostov, a trio of the new Il-2s were hacked down, one each being credited to the *Gruppe's* three top scorers, Köppen, Rall and Graf.

Five days later, after claiming his 36th kill (an I-16 to the north of the city), Oberleutnant Günther Rall was himself seriously injured in an emergency landing. His back broken, it would be nine long months before he returned to operations and resumed command of 8. *Staffel*. In the meantime, a lot was to happen.

On the day of Rall's crash – 28 November 1941 – the Red Army succeeded in re-taking Rostov. III./JG 52 held out at Taganrog for a further fortnight, enduring not only near constant bombing and ground-strafing attacks, but also the attentions of what pilots and groundcrews alike referred to as 'Stalin's secret weapon' – a plague of rats!

It was at this time that Leutnant Hermann Graf, currently with 34 victories under his belt, confided to his diary;

'Only Feldwebel Köppen is ahead of me. Who would have thought I would have got as far as this. Certainly not me! Yesterday, I flew a *freie Jagd* with my friend Grislawski. Over the Mius line a few rickety old I-5 (sic) biplanes were attacking the SS positions. After my first pass one went down, then a second followed. Grislawski even managed to bag three.

'In the evening Sepp Dietreich (*Obergruppenführer der Waffen-SS* Josef 'Sepp' Dietrich, Commander of the SS-Panzerdivision *Leibstandarte Adolf Hitler*) arrived at the field and shook each of us warmly by the hand. He was full of praise and asked if there was anything we needed. We explained that we no longer had any trucks. He promised to send us one. And, sure enough, one duly turned up, loaded with smokes and alcohol!'

With Taganrog becoming untenable, III./JG 52 was transferred to Kharkov on 10 December. Eight days later Feldwebel Gerhard Köppen

8./JG 52's Feldwebel Köppen was the first member of III. *Gruppe* to win the Knight's Cross, awarded on 18 December 1941 for 40 kills. The achievement is marked by the single black victory bar seen here surrounded by 61 white ones – for it is now February 1942 at Kharkov, and Gerhard Köppen is just a few days, and ten more kills, away from the Oak Leaves

was awarded the *Gruppe's* first Knight's Cross – the citation read 'for 40 victories', although by that time his actual score had risen to nearer 50.

III. *Gruppe* would spend the rest of the winter at Kharkov. Hermann Graf was finding less to write about in his diary. On 26 December;

'Christmas! Best not to even think about it. No change to my score (of 37). The opposition has quietened down a lot.'

It was to be the quiet before the storm. On 24 January Leutnant Hermann Graf received the first of 1942's 24(!) Knight's Crosses. Within nine months he would be sporting the Diamonds.

The opening weeks of 1942 saw the weather deteriorate even further. Temperatures continued to drop. There were heavy snow blizzards and days of near zero visibility. After claiming 90 kills without loss in December (making them the top scorers on the southern sector), III./JG 52 reported few contacts with the enemy during January.

By this time its new *Kommandeur* had arrived. Hauptmann Hubertus von Bonin was a veteran of the *Legion Condor* (with four Spanish kills), and more recently had commanded I./JG 54. Under his leadership, III./JG 52 would rise from being the highest-scoring unit in *Luftflotte* 4 to become the most successful *Jagdgruppe* in the entire Luftwaffe.

Despite the atrocious conditions, III./JG 52 managed to add some 40 kills to its scoreboard during the first two months of 1942. As the only *Gruppe* of the three not to be rotated back to the homeland for rest and refit, and with a solid cadre of by now highly experienced pilots, it is perhaps little wonder that all 15 of the high awards won by JG 52 during the first half of 1942 went to members of III. *Gruppe*.

Following Hermann Graf's Knight's Cross of 24 January for 42 kills, Feldwebel Leopold Steinbatz, who was Graf's regular wingman, was similarly honoured on 14 February for achieving the same total. But still in the lead was Feldwebel Gerhard Köppen, who, on 27 February, was honoured with the Oak Leaves – the *Geschwader's* first – for 72 enemy aircraft destroyed.

March 1942 has been described as a month of 'preparation and consolidation' for German forces on the southern sector. III./JG 52's

JG 52's area of operations during the first 18 months of the war on the eastern front (*map by John Weal*)

scores were now rising steadily, resulting in Knight's Crosses for Leutnant Adolf Dickfeld and Feldwebel Edmund Rossmann on 19 March (for 47 and 52 victories respectively).

21 March was officially the first day of spring, but the thermometer was still reading 13 below zero and heavy snow continued to fall. Two days later Oberleutnant Kurt Schade was brought down behind Soviet lines and Leutnant Hermann Graf was appointed *Staffelkapitän* of 9./JG 52 in his place.

The build-up in the south went on throughout April and into May as the Wehrmacht prepared for its 1942 offensive. Unlike the previous year's *Barbarossa*, however, *Fall Blau* (Case 'Blue') was not to be directed against Moscow. Its objective was the oilfields of the Caucasus. Also, it was to be launched in the late spring, a month earlier then *Barbarossa* had been set in motion. The latter's fatal four-week deferment – occasioned by the need to bring the Balkans into line before attacking the Soviet Union – was the main reason why German troops were still short of Moscow when winter closed in.

5 April, the day Adolf Hitler first outlined his plans for *Fall Blau*, saw another Knight's Cross awarded to III./JG 52. This time the recipient was Unteroffizier Friedrich Wachowiak, whose score had reached 46. Forty-eight hours later it was announced that JG 52's collective total had passed the 1000 mark. This achievement was due in no small measure to the victories being racked up by III. *Gruppe*. Since the beginning of *Barbarossa*, 9. *Staffel* alone had been credited with well over 200 kills for just eight losses.

Towards the end of April II./JG 52 returned to the eastern front after nearly three months in Germany. The *Gruppe* was now commanded by

The two Knight's Cross winners of 19 March 1942 are pictured together in this animated group of 7. *Staffel* pilots – Leutnant Adolf Dickfeld (holding map) and Feldwebel Edmund Rossmann (far right). Recognisable between them are Feldwebel Paul Eberhardt (killed in action on 27 November 1943) and, leaning forward, future Oak Leaves winner Feldwebel Josef 'Jupp' Zwernemann

Hauptmann Johannes Steinhoff. The unit's previous *Kommandeur*, Hauptmann Erich Woitke, had reportedly been court-martialled and demoted for having 'failed to respond' to a warning of a Red Army attack on the unit's base back in January which had cost the lives of several pilots and groundcrew members.

On 29 April (the day of II./JG 52's arrival at Kharkov-South), III. *Gruppe* departed Zaporozhe – a field it had been sharing with the *Geschwaderstab* since February – for Zürichtal, in the Crimea. Here, the unit's old friends in 11. *Armee* were preparing an offensive of their own. Code-named *Trappenjagd* ('Bustard Hunt'), its aim was to clear the Crimean peninsula of its last Soviet defenders. The next fortnight would go a long way towards cementing III./JG 52's reputation as the Luftwaffe's highest scoring *Jagdgruppe*.

Operating mainly over Kerch, on the easternmost tip of the Crimea – an area re-occupied by the Red Army during the winter – III. *Gruppe* immediately began to make its presence felt. On 30 April, in the company of II./JG 77, its pilots claimed 24 enemy machines without loss. The following day, starting in the pre-dawn darkness at 0330 hrs, 9. *Staffel* flew no fewer than six separate missions. By its end, Hermann Graf had added six more Soviet aircraft to his score.

Twenty-four hours later he went one better with seven, taking his total to 76. Graf was rapidly catching up with 7. *Staffel's* Gerhard Köppen, whose five victories on 2 May had elevated his score to 84. But it was fate that decided the outcome of the contest on 5 May when Leutnant Köppen was forced to ditch in the Sea of Azov, just north of the Kerch Straits, after attacking two Pe-2s. He was spotted swimming for shore, and it is believed that he was picked up by a Soviet vessel. Köppen was not seen again.

Trappenjagd kicked off on 8 May. On that date II. *Gruppe* flew into the Crimea to help support 11. *Armee's* drive on Kerch. The day also saw Hermann Graf add another eight aircraft to his lengthening list of kills, and the *Geschwader's* overall total climb to 1500.

On 7 April 1942 it was announced that JG 52 had reached an overall total of 1000 enemy aircraft destroyed. Some 46 of that number were credited to 8. *Staffel's* Unteroffizier Friedrich Wachowiak (hands in pockets), for which he had been awarded the Knight's Cross two days earlier

A smiling Friedrich Wachowiak (right) – perhaps about to go on a spot of leave in that transport He 111 in the background – proudly sports his new feldwebel insignia and recently-won Knight's Cross. This shot must have been taken within a month of the award, for his equally happy companion – the now Oberfeldwebel Gerhard Köppen, Oak Leaves hidden by his gloved hand – would be reported missing on 5 May 1942

Although photographed later in the year, this quartet of III. *Gruppe* stalwarts shown here includes Oberfeldwebel Ernst Süss (far left), who was reportedly responsible for 9. *Staffel's* famous name which was adopted during its two-week stint in the Crimea in the spring of 1942. The *Kapitän* of 9./JG 52, Oberleutnant Hermann Graf, is holding the hound. Flanking him are 7. *Staffel's* Hans Dammers (left) and 'Jupp' Zwernemann (right)

Fall Blau was nearing launch too, but Soviet intelligence had learned of the coming offensive, and the Red Army staged an ambitious spoiling attack to the south of Kharkov. Its aim was to cut off the German forces assembling for the advance down into the Caucasus from the main body of the front. This sudden threat resulted in III./JG 52 being rushed back to Kharkov-Rogan on 12 May.

During its two weeks in the Crimea, 9./JG 52 had been the most successful of the *Gruppe's* three *Staffeln*, destroying 93 enemy aircraft without loss. It also gained the famous name by which it is still known to this day. Future Knight's Cross winner Oberfeldwebel Ernst Süss had returned from leave clutching a portable record player. Unfortunately, none of the records he brought with him survived the journey from East

Prussia. The only thing he had to play was a Russian record picked up locally, and the lyrics on this disc kept repeating a phrase which, to Süss's ears, sounded something like 'Karaya, Karaya'. Soon, the whole *Staffel* was familiar with the tune. Süss even sang it loudly over the R/T while on ops. It did not take long for *'Karaya'* to become 9./JG 52's official radio call sign.

The huge battle fought around the Izyum pocket to the south of Kharkov, where German forces first halted and then smashed the Soviet breakthrough attempt, would last from 17 to 28 May. Its successful outcome cleared the way for *Fall Blau*. But it is also of some significance to the story of JG 52 as it was here, for one of the very few times in its history, that the entire *Geschwader* would operate together from the same base.

II./JG 52 had quickly followed III. *Gruppe* back up from the Crimea, taking up residence at Artemovsk, a large airfield in the Donetz basin some 125 miles (200 km) south-southeast of Kharkov, on 15 May. It was joined there by the *Geschwaderstab* and I. *Gruppe* (the latter just back from Germany) five days later. Twenty-four hours after that, III./JG 52 completed the line-up by flying in to Artemovsk from Kharkov-Rogan.

For JG 52, the fighting around Kharkov would put even III. *Gruppe's* recent Crimean successes in the shade.

From this point onwards it would be all too easy to allow the story of the *Geschwader's* final three years to degenerate into a mere list of names and numbers, as individual and collective scores climbed into the hundreds and thousands respectively. But such a catalogue would soon become both repetitive and tedious. It is also well beyond the scope of a limited work of this nature. The *Geschwader's* performance in the Kharkov battle, and its aftermath, warrants telling in some detail, however, as it so aptly sets the pattern for the months to come – not just the soaring rate of claims, but also the attendant, and growing, number of casualties.

III./JG 52 had been credited with 89 victories in their first two days at Kharkov-Rogan (which took its overall total beyond 1000). Thirteen of these had fallen to Leutnant Hermann Graf, bringing his personal score to 104. He thus became the first member of JG 52 to achieve the century, for which he was awarded the Oak Leaves – a substantial increase on the 72

The tail of Hermann Graf's 'Yellow 1' displays the 104 (or is it 106?) victories which won him the Oak Leaves and Swords within 48 hours of each other. This photograph was taken at Kharkov-Rogan in May 1942

Oberleutnant Graf's decorations are on display in this informal shot of him surrounded by pilots of his *'Karaya' Staffel*. Note the tail of the oddly-camouflaged Polikarpov U-2 in the left background – in all likelihood a captured specimen used as a unit runabout

kills which had won Gerhard Köppen the same honour back in February! Leutnant Adolf Dickfeld was not far behind Graf, nine victories on 14 May having raised his tally to 90. Then, an unprecedented 11 kills in a single day – 18 May – took him past the century too. Dickfeld received the Oak Leaves 24 hours later.

By that same 19 May Hermann Graf had added just two more Soviet aircraft to his previous score of 104. Such were the seeming vagaries of the awards system at this time, however, that this duo promptly won Graf the Swords! By the time he departed for the Führer's HQ for the presentation ceremony two days later, he had at least downed a couple more Red Air Force machines.

Even the recently arrived I. *Gruppe* was getting in on the act. Still lagging badly in the scoring stakes, its pilots nonetheless claimed '13 for 0' in their first three days at Artemovsk, and by 26 May had surpassed the

While re-equipping in Germany, I./JG 52 had taken delivery of its first Bf 109F-4/R1 'gunboats'. One such is pictured here (right), its underwing MG 151/15 cannon gondola clearly visible, at Olmütz (Olomouc), in Czechoslovakia, during the *Gruppe's* return to the eastern front. Given the amount of timber used in the construction of the hangar, the large *Rauchen Verboten* (No Smoking) sign stretching across the width of its back wall was perhaps a wise precaution

300 mark. That day also saw II. *Gruppe's* Johannes Steinhoff increase his tally to 60.

Despite the fact that all Soviet resistance on the ground south of Kharkov had ceased by 21 May, there was little evidence of a let-up in aerial activity. On 2 June Graf's wingman, Oberfeldwebel Leopold Steinbatz, was awarded the Oak Leaves for his 83 victories. But the day was completely overshadowed by the loss of *Geschwaderkommodore* Major Wilhelm Lessmann, whose Bf 109 took a direct hit from an anti-aircraft shell. This event cast a pall over the next day's announcement that JG 52 had achieved its collective 2000th enemy aircraft destroyed.

There were two more major losses before June was out. After claiming three Soviet machines in quick succession near Volzhansk on 15 June (which left him just one short of his century), Leopold Steinbatz also fell victim to Soviet anti-aircraft fire. The 11th ranking fighter pilot at the time of his death, 'Bazi' Steinbatz was honoured with posthumous Swords (and promotion to leutnant) on 23 June. He was the first NCO in the entire Wehrmacht (German armed forces) to be accorded this prestigious award. Also on 23 June another of III. *Gruppe's* Oberfeldwebeln, Josef 'Jupp' Zwernemann, received the Knight's Cross for 57 victories.

Forty-eight hours prior to this, however, Major Lessmann's short-lived successor, Oberstleutnant Friedrich Beckh – previously the *Kommodore* of JG 51 – had been reported missing after ground-strafing Red Army positions near Kupyansk, to the east of Kharkov. It is believed that he made an emergency landing behind enemy lines, but like so many pilots

On 23 June 1942 Oberleutnant Josef Zwernemann received the Knight's Cross for a score of 57. Typical of the veteran NCOs who formed the backbone of III./JG 52, the then Oberfeldwebel Zwernemann's first kill had been a Spitfire off Margate (one of only four confirmed victories credited to the *Gruppe* during the Battle of Britain). 'Jupp' Zwernemann would lose his life as an oberleutnant and *Staffelkapitän* of 1./JG 11 in action against P-51s over Germany on 8 April 1944

While it was the pilots who gained the recognition and the awards, they could not have done so without the untiring efforts of the groundcrews – as the pilots themselves were always the first to acknowledge. The unsung heroes who toiled on the ground almost invariably remain unidentified. But the photographer who snapped this trio on the wing of one of I./JG 52's 'gunboats' made a point of recording their names – Haas, Bertl and Steinmann – as a tribute to the many thousands of otherwise unknowns

who fell into Soviet hands, there was no further trace of him. Beckh's place at the head of the *Geschwader* was taken by the Swords-wearing, 100-victory *Experte* Hauptmann (later Major) Herbert Ihlefeld, hitherto the *Kommandeur* of I./JG 77.

On 28 June *Fall Blau* finally got underway. Along a front stretching some 500 miles (800 km) from Kursk down to the Sea of Azov, eight German and Axis satellite armies – nearly three-and-a-half million men in all – began the advance that was intended to expand Hitler's domain to the banks of the

But sometimes even the 'black men' had the chance of a break. This cheerful bunch have decided to spend theirs queueing for the hairdresser – his barber's chair a pile of cartridge boxes – while another of their number puts the finishing touches to 5. *Staffel's* 'Black 12' in the background

Hauptmann Herbert Ihlefeld (in the leather flight jacket) assumed command of JG 52 after his predecessor, Oberstleutnant Friedrich Beckh, failed to return from a ground-strafing sortie east of Kharkov on 21 June 1942

Volga, and present him with Caucasia's oil. To provide effective support for this immense concentration of ground strength, the southern sector's *Luftflotte* 4 would have needed to be four times its actual size. With only 150 serviceable machines, its single-engined fighter component would be particularly overstretched. And with the Red Air Force growing stronger by the day – both in quality and quantity – the balance of air power on the eastern front was subtly, but perceptibly, changing. It may only have been faint, but the writing was already on the wall.

Groundcrews took great pride in the successes of 'their' pilots. Here, kill number 45 is added to the rudder of Oberleutnant Siegfried Simsch's 'Black 1'. This total earned the *Staffelkapitän* of 5./JG 52 the Knight's Cross on 1 July 1942

Two other recipients of the Knight's Cross on 1 July were Unteroffizier Karl 'Charlie' Gratz of 8. *Staffel*, who would end the war a leutnant with 138 kills to his credit . . .

. . . and 9. *Staffel's* Feldwebel Karl Steffen, who was one of the many members of JG 52 that would disappear for ever after coming down behind enemy lines. Steffen forced-landed southwest of Byelgorod on 8 August 1943 with his score standing at 59

JG 52 supported the opening phase of the advance from its airfields to the east of Kharkov. There was no shortage of opposition. On 1 July – by which time *Blau* had already been renamed *Braunschweig* ('Brunswick') – four more members of the *Geschwader* received the Knight's Cross (for scores ranging from 40 to 54). Although this quartet were all members of either II. and III. *Gruppen* (see Appendix 2), I./JG 52 was gaining ground, and reached its 500 a week later.

On 10 July, while the fighting was still raging – over the past 72 hours *Luftflotte* 4's fighters had shot down 92 Soviet aircraft and destroyed a

When III./JG 52 re-equipped with Bf 109Gs in July 1942, it would appear that they finally abandoned the oversized wavy bar *Gruppe* symbol which had been such a distinctive feature on all their machines since the unit's activation back in March 1940. Note also the dappled engine cowling as worn by a number of early *Gustavs* on the eastern front

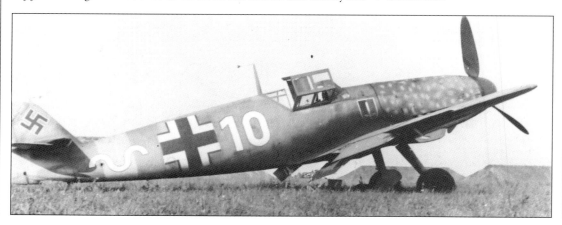

II. *Gruppe's* first Bf 109Gs, many of which displayed dense dappling on their cowlings, introduced a fundamental change in the unit's markings. For the first time in their history the aircraft of II./JG 52 now sported a standard horizontal bar II. *Gruppe* symbol on their aft fuselages, as seen here on *Gruppenkommandeur* Hauptmann Johannes Steinhhoff's 'Black Double Chevron'. For some reason II./JG 52 had studiously ignored this regulation in the past . . .

. . . and while on the subject of non-conformity, Hauptmann Helmut Bennemann, recently appointed *Kommandeur* of I. *Gruppe*, appears to have very definite ideas of his own as to what constitutes a good camouflage scheme! Just what colours he is instructing the mechanic to apply to the cowling of his 'gunboat' is anybody's guess!

further 35 on the ground – Major von Bonin's III. *Gruppe* was pulled back to Kharkov to begin conversion onto Bf 109Gs. Ten days later it was the turn of I./G 52 to hand its remaining *Friedrichs* over to II. *Gruppe* and retire to Kharkov for similar re-equipment, Hauptmann Steinhoff's pilots would have to soldier on a little longer before they too converted to the *Gustav*.

The *Geschwader* was fortunate not to lose its third Kommodore in the space of less than two months when Major Ihlefeld was caught in his *Storch* by Red Air Force fighters on 22 July. Despite being seriously wounded, he survived the attack.

The following day Adolf Hitler made a fatal decision. The southern offensive was no longer to advance across a broad front. Instead, he

directed that its forces be split in half and sent against two entirely separate objectives. While Army Group 'A' pushed south-eastwards down into the Caucasus, Army Group 'B' would strike due east for Stalingrad. The widely divergent axes of advance of the two Army Groups was a recipe for military disaster.

It also heralded another parting of the ways for JG 52. The *Geschwader* was currently deployed in its entirety around Rostov-on-Don, but now II. and III. *Gruppen* were scheduled to accompany Army Group 'A' down into the vastness of the Caucasus, while I./JG 52 was given the role of 'fire brigade' unit. Rarely again would JG 52's component parts operate in such close proximity to each other, for even though II. and III./JG 52 would both be in the Caucasus, such was the area to be covered – and so far apart would the ground armies' spearheads be – that the two *Gruppen* could be separated by as much as 300 miles (480 km). Even individual *Staffeln* were soon being detached to operate semi-autonomously from their own forward landing grounds.

By the latter half of August, for example, while II./JG 52 was supporting 17. *Armee's* drive towards the oil wells of Maikop, in the northwest foothills of the Caucasus mountains, III. *Gruppe* was covering 1. *Panzerarmee's* continuing thrust southeast towards the oilfields closer to the shores of the Caspian. Meanwhile, I./JG 52 found itself attached to JG 51 and based near Rzhev, some 105 miles (170 km) to the west of Moscow!

A typical landing ground 'somewhere in the south' during III. *Gruppe's* push down into the wastes of the Caucasus in the late summer of 1942. Note the wide dispersal of the individual machines – dictated by the threat of enemy air attack – and compare this desolate expanse with the bustle at Lepel a year earlier as seen in the photograph on page 58

Bare fields such as that above offered few, if any, amenities for the hard-pressed 'black men'. But as long as the weather remained good, they could at least carry on working out in the open. Here, an engine is given an overhaul while, in the foreground, the contents of the coolant header tank are drained into a bucket

The month's four Knight's Crosses were all awarded on 23 August. One went to Oberleutnant Gerhard Barkhorn, the *Staffelkapitän* of 4./JG 52, for his 59 victories. Another was presented posthumously to I. *Gruppe's* Oberfeldwebel Heinz-Wilhelm Ahnert, who had been shot down that very day while attacking a formation of Pe-2s near Orel, in the central sector.

On 27 August German forces captured the town of Mozdok, on the banks of the River Terek. This was the last water barrier between them and the first of the Caspian oilfields less than 75 miles (120 km) away, around Grozny. But the Terek also represented the farthestmost point that Hitler's troops would reach in their invasion of the Soviet Union. For the remainder of the year the Red Army would defend this river line with a grim tenacity that was to be completely overshadowed by an even greater struggle developing 425 miles (680 km) to the north – the battle for Stalingrad.

The day after the fall of Mozdok, Oberleutnant Günther Rall arrived at Gostanovka, III./JG 52's forward airstrip close to the Terek, to re-assume command of his 8. *Staffel*. It was exactly nine months since Rall had broken his back in a crash-landing. It says as much for his powers of recuperation, as it does about the level of aerial activity along the Terek, that it took Rall less than a week to raise his previous score of 36 to 65, for which he received the Knight's Cross on 3 September.

A number of the other awards were presented during the first week of September. Among them was the Oak Leaves for Hauptmann Johannes Steinhoff, who had claimed his 100th victory on 31 August. And of

Proving that a *Staffelkapitän's* work is never done either, 4./JG 52's Hauptmann Gerhard Barkhorn – just back from patrol, still in flying gear and wearing the Knight's Cross awarded on 23 August 1942 – gets down to some urgent business on the telephone

Recently returned to ops nine months after breaking his back in a crash-landing, Oberleutnant Günther Rall also sports a newly-won Knight's Cross. Seen with him in front of 'Black 13' are two veteran NCOs – 'Charlie' Gratz (left) and Friedrich Wachowiak (right) – of his *Staffel*, each of whom had been similarly decorated during his enforced absence

4 September's two Knight's Crosses, one was posthumous and the other went to Oberfeldwebel Ernst Süss (of *'Karaya'* fame) for 50 enemy aircraft destroyed. It was also on 4 September that the Kapitän of the *'Karaya' Staffel*, Oberleutnant Hermann Graf, became the second fighter pilot in history to achieve 150 victories.

In fact, since mid-August 9./JG 52 (together with 6. *Staffel*) had been detached to form the so-called Stalingrad-*Kommando*, which was operating under the control of JG 3 in support of 6. *Armee's* still leisurely advance across the Don Bend towards Stalin's namesake city on the Volga. On 13 September the *Kommando* moved to Pitomnik, the airfield just nine miles (15 km) west of Stalingrad which would be used to evacuate the wounded during the beleaguered city's final death-throes.

But there were no indications of the horrors Pitomnik was to witness in the depths of the coming winter when, on 16 September, Hermann Graf

But it was fellow *Staffelkapitän* Oberleutnant Hermann Graf of 9./JG 52 who was still the *Geschwader's* top scorer. On 4 September Graf became only the second pilot in the entire *Jagdwaffe* to reach a total of 150 kills (just six days behind JG 77's Major Gordon M Gollob). The achievement was duly marked on the rudder of Graf's 'Yellow 1'. And more victory bars were soon being added as Graf surged towards the 172 which would win him the Diamonds

claimed victory number 172 to become the Luftwaffe's top-scoring pilot. This feat was recognised by much fanfare, and the award of the Diamonds. On the same day II. *Gruppe's* Leutnant Heinz Schmidt, who had won the Knight's Cross on 23 August for 51 victories, received the Oak Leaves for reaching 102. It had taken 'Johnny' Schmidt 14 months to amass those first 51 kills, and he had doubled them in a little over three weeks – another indication, if any were needed, of the ferocity of the air war in the south during the early autumn of 1942.

But it was Hermann Graf who was attracting all the attention. Replaced at Pitomnik by I. *Gruppe* (which would remain in the Stalingrad area until early November), the *Kommando* returned to the Terek front on 28 September. And it was here, four days later, that Hauptmann Hermann Graf became the first fighter pilot in the world to reach the double century. This earned him promotion to major, and an immediate ban on all further combat flying.

Apart from the sole example of the Golden Oak Leaves with Swords and Diamonds (awarded to only one man, Stuka ace Hans-Ulrich Rudel), the Diamonds were the Third Reich's highest military decoration. They were bestowed only 27 times during the course of the war, with exactly one-third of that number going to fighter pilots. Graf was the fifth pilot to be so honoured. But the pilots of the *'Karaya' Staffel* hardly had time to register the fact before their *Kapitän* was taken off ops and returned to the Reich.

Uniquely, however, JG 52 was to be the only *Jagdgeschwader* to produce *two* winners of the Diamonds. And although nobody of course realised it at the time, the second of them had arrived on the scene just six days after Major Graf's departure.

It was on 8 October that four replacement leutnants reported to *Geschwader* HQ outside Maikop to receive the usual introductory

A smiling Oberleutnant Hermann Graf poses for the camera amidst a jubilant crowd of III. *Gruppe* pilots and groundcrew. Among the familiar names in the front row are, from right to left, Süss, Gratz, Rossmann, Graf, Steffen and Zwernemann. The *Geschwader's* own Junkers W 34 transport (note its 'winged sword' badge beneath the cocpkit) waiting in the background – passenger door open and pilot perched in the cockpit hatch – would seem to suggest that Graf is about to leave for Germany, and the presentation of the Diamonds

pep-talk from acting-*Kommodore* Major Dietrich Hrabak. After the formalities were over, Hrabak assigned all four to III. *Gruppe*, currently based at Soldatskaya – another forward landing ground close to the Terek. Here, *Gruppenkommandeur* Hubertus von Bonin split them up, sending one pair to Graf's 9. *Staffel* (now led by Hauptmann Ernst Ehrenberg) and the other to 7. *Staffel*, which was headed by Hauptmann Adalbert Sommer.

Of the latter two, one would be killed within the month. The other – whose slender, fair-haired figure and youthful looks quickly earned him the nickname *'Bubi'* ('Sonny') – would not simply survive the war. He would emerge from it as the highest-scoring fighter pilot of all time.

But first Leutnant Erich Hartmann had to be taught the ropes of combat flying. In III./JG 52 (as indeed in practically every other *Jagdgruppe* in the Luftwaffe) rank gave way to experience when operations were being flown. Even *Kommandeur* von Bonin deferred to this unwritten rule, acting as *Katschmarek* – the pilots' own term for a wingman or number two – to the more experienced Leutnant Alfred Grislawski, one of 1 July's quartet of Knight's Cross winners.

Other awards were made nearer to home. Here, Major Hubertus von Bonin (right), *Gruppenkommandeur* of III./JG 52, presents the Knight's Cross 'in the field' to Feldwebel Alfred Grislawski, the highly experienced 9. *Staffel* NCO who was soon to be commisssioned and would lead the *Stabsschwarm* in the air, with von Bonin flying as *his* number two

III. *Gruppe* possessed a valuable core of veteran NCOs who flew as *Schwarmführer* (leaders of four-aircraft elements), not simply to protect their less experienced superiors, but also – and much more importantly – to impart their knowledge and skills to a constant stream of replacement pilots. Two such stalwarts are pictured here – Oberfeldwebel Edmund 'Paule' Rossmann (left) and Feldwebel Hans Dammers (right). One of the former's protégés was a certain fresh-faced youngster named Erich Hartmann

Erich Hartmann's mentor was veteran NCO and *Schwarmführer* Feldwebel Edmund Rossmann, another Knight's Cross holder with more than 80 kills to his credit. It was Rossmann's expertise and patient tutelage which enabled the young leutnant to develop his own winning formula for success in the air; see – decide – attack – break away.

While Erich Hartmann was learning his craft under the wing (both figuratively and literally) of 'Paule' Rossmann, the more established members of the *Geschwader* continued to add to their growing list of kills. October saw the awarding of four more Knight's Crosses, all for 50 kills or more. And there were also Oak Leaves for two new centurions. Oberleutnant Günther Rall had arrived at his 100 with the third of a trio of LaGGs downed on 22 October, for which he was decorated six days later. And on the last day of the month Oberfeldwebel 'Jupp' Zwernemann reached 101.

On 1 November Major Dietrich Hrabak officially assumed command of JG 52 from the injured Herbert Ihlefeld. By this time 6. *Armee* was fighting desperately amongst the rubble of Stalingrad as the battle for the ruined city approached its climax. But Hauptmann Bennemann's I./JG 52 at Pitomnik was spared the fate awaiting General von Paulus' ground troops. On 5 November the *Gruppe* was ordered to hand over its remaining *Gustavs* to JG 3 and retire to Rostov for re-equipment.

It was also on 5 November that Leutnant Erich Hartmann claimed his first victory down in the Caucasus. He was one of the *Alarmschwarm*, led by the Adjutant of III. *Gruppe*, Leutnant Rudolf Trepte, which was hastily scrambled to meet an incoming raid of 18 *Sturmoviks*, escorted by some dozen LaGG-3 fighters – four against thirty!

Trying to remember everything that had been drummed into him in the past weeks, Hartmann dived steeply on one of the dark green *Sturmoviks*.

Higher up the chain of command, JG 52 officially welcomed its sixth, and penultimate, *Kommodore* on 1 November 1942. Arriving from II./JG 54, a *Gruppe* he had led since August 1940, Major Dietrich Hrabak would remain at the head of the *Geschwader* for almost two years. He is seen here (centre, pointing) with pilots of III./JG 52, among them (to his immediate right) Josef Zwernemann and Günther Rall

But on his first pass his bullets – even his cannon shells – bounced harmlessly off the Soviet machine's armoured hide. A second dive took him down almost to ground level, below and behind the formation of weaving Ilyushins. Utilising his excess speed, he came up beneath them, closing in to about 200 ft (60 m) before opening fire. This time he was rewarded by a tongue of flame blowtorching out of his victim.

Forgetting all Rossmann's advice in the heat of the moment, Hartmann followed the stricken *Sturmovik* down in a shallow dive. It was his undoing. A large piece of metal broke off the Ilyushin's wing and smashed into his own machine. With smoke filling his cockpit, Hartmann fought the *Gustav* down into a spectacular crash-landing. Just over a mile (1.6 km) away, his first kill smashed into the ground and exploded. It would be nearly three months before he claimed his second. And during that time the situation on the eastern front was to change dramatically.

On 9 November Hauptmann Steinhoff's II. *Gruppe* returned from a brief deployment on the Terek front to rejoin the *Geschwaderstab* at Maikop. Its task was to protect that area's oil wells, which German engineers were still struggling to get back into production after the damage inflicted by the retreating Russians in August. It was at this juncture that the third squadron of foreign volunteers – Slovakian-manned 13.(*slow*)/JG 52 – to serve under JG 52 on the eastern front was attached to II. *Gruppe* (see *Osprey Aircraft of the Aces 58 - Slovakian and Bulgarian Aces of World War 2* for further details).

Then the blow fell. On 19 November the Red Army launched massive counter-offensives on either side of Stalingrad that quickly threatened to encircle and entrap the whole of 6. *Armee* within the city. II./JG 52 was quickly moved up to the Don, southwest of Stalingrad, where the Rumanian 4th Army was coming under great pressure from the advancing Soviets. But it was too late. The 6. *Armee* was already trapped, and in danger of slow annihilation unless the Führer authorised a break-out. This he flatly refused to do.

'Black Chevron 1' was the mount of Leutnant Rudolf Trepte, *Gruppen-Adjutant* of III./JG 52. The fighter is seen here having its engine topped up with oil prior to its next mission. Leutnant Erich Hartmann claimed the first of his 352 kills while flying as a member of Trepte's *Schwarm* on 5 November 1942

Late 1942 on the southwest Stalingrad front. A *Rotte* (two-aircraft element) of 4./JG 52 churns across a field of snow to the compacted stretch of runway beyond (marked in the right background by the line of small evergreen branches). Other lessons have also been learned from the winter before. Note, for example, how the undercarriage leg fairings have been removed to prevent a dangerous build-up of snow and ice between fairings and mainwheels, which could easily flip a machine on to its back

II. *Gruppe* would remain on the southwest Stalingrad front until the end of the year. And despite the rapidly worsening situation on all sectors, the *Geschwader* continued to take its toll of the Red Air Force. Having claimed a staggering 2000 victories over the previous six months, JG 52 was credited with its 4000th enemy aircraft destroyed on 10 December.

Forty-eight hours later, 4. *Panzerarmee* launched an attempt to open a corridor through to the besieged defenders of Stalingrad from the southwest. II./JG 52 moved up to an airfield within 90 miles (150 km) of the city in support, but this was to no avail. The three Panzer divisions spearheading the relief force could not break the solid ring of steel surrounding 6. *Armee*.

On 19 December, southwest of Stalingrad, Oberleutnant Gerhard Barkhorn, *Staffelkapitän* of 4./JG 52, claimed his 100th kill. By this stage, however, the century no longer automatically guaranteed the Oak Laves, and Barkhorn would have to wait another three weeks, and add a further 20 kills to his score, before he won the award. It was *Kommodore* Major von Bonin down in Maikop who received the *Geschwader's* last decoration of the year – the Knight's Cross on 21 December for 51 victories.

With 4. *Panzer-Armee's* rescue attempt brought to a halt just 30 miles (48 km) short of the Stalingrad perimeter on 24 December, the 6. *Armee's* fate was sealed. The southern arm of the Soviet counter-offensive began to push along the line of the Don towards Rostov. A catastrophe even greater than Stalingrad was now looming. If the Russians reached the Sea of Azov, the whole of Army Group 'A' down in the Caucasus would be cut off.

The pilots of Johannes Steinhoff's II./JG 52 finally evacuated their base at Kotelnikovski, to the south-west of Stalingrad, on 27 December when Soviet tanks were reported to be less than two-and-a-half miles (four kilometres) away. After a night of bombardment, the groundcrews left by road at first light the following morning. In temperatures of 30 degrees below zero, they set out on the 150-mile (240-km) journey to Salsk, a field in the northern Caucasus, east-southeast of Rostov. They were joined there by III. *Gruppe*, which had also been forced to abandon their forward landing ground at Soldatskaya on the Terek.

The whole of Army Group 'A' was now withdrawing to escape entrapment by the westward advance of the Russians. The Terek had marked the high-water mark of Hitler's incursion into the Soviet Union. Now the tide was turning – a tide of Red Army units that soon became a torrent, and then a flood which would ultimately engulf the Führer's own capital city, Berlin.

EASTERN FRONT – RETREAT

The 1942 summer offensive had failed on both counts. Stalingrad had not fallen, and the Caucasian oil wells had not been captured. Now it was the turn of the Red Army to take the initiative. It was the beginning of the end for Germany and her eastern satellites, who were to be forced into an accelerating succession of withdrawals, holding actions, abortive counter-offensives, and retreats as they were driven back over the very same ground across which they had advanced with such *élan* only the year before.

For JG 52 this would mean abandoning the Caucasus and Crimea, and retiring back through the Ukraine into Rumania – its main jumping-off point for *Barbarossa* – and beyond, to Czechoslovakia, Austria and, finally, into Germany itself. Ironically, it was during this final, fraught chapter in the *Geschwader's* history, while almost constantly on the defensive, that its pilots achieved their greatest numerical successes. Before the final surrender, they were to add well over 6000 aircraft destroyed to the 4000 already claimed.

The first priority of 1943 was to extricate Army Group 'A' from the Caucasus. 1. *Panzer-Armee* on the eastern flank was in the most danger of being cut off, and II. and III./JG 52 were therefore moved to Rostov. Here, but for a few brief redeployments, they would remain for over a month to protect the army's units as they retreated northwards and

Despite the tide of war turning slowly but steadily against them, the pilots of JG 52 continued to give their all. This unidentified Oberfeldwebel of 5. *Staffel* smiles broadly as he clutches a garland in one hand and a bottle in the other. The reason for the celebration? Just visible on the original print, the placard held in front of 'Black 3' reads, 'Heartiest congratulations on your 400th mission' . . .

streamed across the Don on either side of the city to the (temporary) safety of the Ukraine.

Meanwhile, 17. *Armee* had been staging a fighting withdrawal back up along the Black Sea coast to the Kuban peninsula in the northwest Caucasus. Still harbouring forlorn hopes of a renewed offensive to capture those elusive Caspian oilfields, Hitler ordered the *Armee* to defend this foothold at all costs. This it would do until finally forced to retreat across the Straits of Kerch to the Crimea in the autumn. The slowly shrinking Kuban bridgehead was to be the scene of many of JG 52's victories in the months to come. It was over Armavir on 27 January, for example, that Leutnant Erich Hartmann was to gain his second kill (a MiG-3), and begin his rise to fame.

But it was the 'fire brigade' I. *Gruppe* up on the Kharkov front which had won the first two Knight's Crosses of the New Year. Both had been awarded on 5 January to members of 2./JG 52 – *Staffelkapitän* Hauptmann Johannes Wiese and Feldwebel Wilhelm Freuwörth, for 51 and 56 kills respectively. Six days later fellow *Staffelkapitän* Oberleutnant Gerhard Barkhorn of 4./JG 52 at last received his Oak Leaves (for 120 kills).

During the latter half of January 1943, I./JG 52 was itself twice nearly overrun. On the first occasion the groundcrews were able to escape Rossosh' by truck while the airfield's flak defences held Red Army tanks and infantry at bay. Four days later they had an even closer call when Soviet cavalry suddenly appeared out of the woods, surrounding their new base at Urasovo.

For four days the encircled *Gruppe* held out against growing numbers of enemy troops, backed up by heavy mortars. Then, Hauptmann Bennemann ordered his pilots to take off, each with his chief mechanic crammed into the rear fuselage of his *Gustav*. With only one transport Ju 52/3m available, the remaining groundcrews were as good as lost. But again their own flak gunners came to the rescue, remaining at their posts while the ground personnel slipped away on foot. After a three-day march through deep snow in temperatures of -25 degrees, the exhausted column reached the nearest army unit, which by then was almost 75 miles (120 km) away.

By early February I. *Gruppe's* pilots and groundcrews were reunited at Kharkov-North. But against mounting Soviet pressure, the city of Kharkov

. . . and many of the missions being flown at this time were to protect the retreating ground troops from attack by Red Air Force *Sturmoviks*. These stills from a German wartime newsreel, although of very poor quality, vividly portray the immediacy of such an action. Responding to a call for help from the ground, a *Schwarm* closes in on one of the enemy . . .

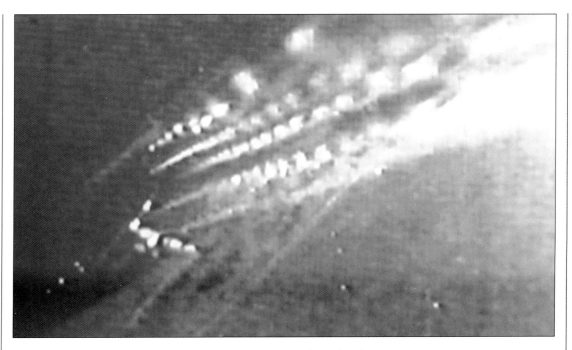

... which desperately tries to evade the hail of cannon fire from the 'gunboat' on its tail. But one of the projectiles finds its mark and ...

itself was abandoned by the *Waffen-SS* (strictly against the Führer's orders) on 16 February, only to be retaken again exactly one month later. Operating out of airfields in the Kharkov-Byelgorod-Poltava triangle, I./JG 52 would remain heavily engaged in this area until mid-May.

Meanwhile, the rest of the *Geschwader* was supporting 17. *Armee's* stubborn defence of the Kuban bridgehead. *Kommodore* Hrabak's *Stab* took up residence on one of the forward landing grounds grouped around Kerch, on the easternmost tip of the Crimean peninsula, on 15 February. It was joined there by II. *Gruppe* the following day.

One of II./JG 52's initial tasks was to mount standing patrols (usually in *Schwarm* strength) over the Straits of Kerch, where small naval units were shuttling back and forth through the drift ice taking supplies into the Kuban and evacuating 17. *Armee's* wounded. Mustering on average less than two-dozen serviceable machines, the *Gruppe* continued to add to its

... trailing a bright banner of flame, the *Sturmovik* goes down vertically, crashing into no-man's land just in front of a German army unit dug in around a Russian farm house

91

list of kills, but was finding it increasingly difficult to protect the ground troops from near constant attack by marauding bands of *Sturmoviks*.

On 11 March Oberfeldwebel Willi 'Old Father' Nemitz, who had recently assumed command of 6. *Staffel* (despite his NCO rank), was awarded the Knight's Cross for 54 victories. Three days later another Knight's Cross, this time posthumous, went to his immediate predecessor, Oberleutnant Gustav Denk, whose Bf 109G had exploded in mid-air after receiving a direct hit while ground-strafing over the Kuban the previous month. Willi Nemitz would himself be killed in combat with Soviet fighters in the same area on 11 April. *His* posthumous reward was promotion to leutnant.

In the second week of March the marshy Kuban's notoriously waterlogged landing grounds were beginning to dry out after the spring thaw. II. *Gruppe* made the short hop across the Straits of Kerch to Anapa, on the Taman peninsula, on 13 March. Its place at Kerch IV was briefly taken by III./JG 52, before it too moved to Taman, on the eastern shores of the straits, on 1 April. The *Geschwaderstab* joined III. *Gruppe* at Taman nine days later. On 16 May I./JG 52 also flew in to Anapa from Kharkov-South, and for the following six weeks, until early July, JG 52 would concentrate all its efforts on supporting the hard-pressed 17. *Armee*.

On 24 March the long-serving Major Johannes Steinhoff said his farewells to II./JG 52. Having claimed his 150th kill during the *Gruppe's* recent stint around Kharkov, 'Mäcki' Steinhoff was now departing to take command of JG 77 in the Mediterranean. His replacement at the head of II./JG 52 was Hauptmann Helmut Kühle.

The *Geschwader's* time in the Kuban bridgehead saw its lengthening scoresheet tempered by an increasing number of losses. One of the 56 enemy aircraft claimed over the Black Sea port of Novorossisk on 20 April gave JG 52 its 5000th victory of the war. On a more personal level, the last day of the month provided Erich Hartmann with his first double. Numbers 10 and 11 were a pair of LaGG-3s brought down near Taman.

Mystery partially solved! On page 67 of *Osprey Aircraft of the Aces 37 - Bf 109 Aces of the Russian Front*, a picture was published showing Erich Hartmann's 'White 2' down behind enemy lines and billowing black smoke. Although it was known that Unteroffizier Herbert Meissler, not Hartmann, had been piloting the machine on the day it went missing (28 May 1943), the exact circumstances were unclear. Firstly, as proof that the G-4/R6 really *was* Erich Hartmann's regular mount, he is pictured here leaning on the tail of the *Gustav*, with its 15 kill bars clearly displayed . . .

. . . and sitting in the cockpit with the first letter of its original code (KJ+GU) and part of the white numeral '2' just visible . . .

But it was the growing list of casualties, particularly among experienced formation leaders, which was beginning to give rise to concern. On 8 April Leutnant Helmut Haberda, *Kapitän* of 5./JG 52 was killed in a dogfight. Forty-eight hours later another *Staffelkapitän* – 9./JG 52's Hauptmann Ernst Ehrenberg, who had taken over the *'Karayas'* from Hermann Graf – was lost. On that same 10 May Major Helmut Bennemann, *Kommandeur* of I./JG 52, was so severely wounded that he could no longer lead the *Gruppe*.

And so it went on. Willi Nemitz's successor at the head of 6. *Staffel*, Oberleutnant Karl Ritzenberger, lasted just over a month. He was shot down by a Yak over Novorossisk on 24 May. Knight's Cross holder Oberleutnant Rudolf Miethig, the *Kapitän* of 3./JG 52, was killed in the resulting crash when he claimed his 101st victory by ramming on 10 June. In all, the *Geschwader's* casualties from April to June totalled 23 pilots killed or missing, plus 14 wounded.

. . . finally, the machine on the ground – obviously intact – and in Russian hands. It had been forced down by pilots of the Soviet 812 Fighter Regiment. Now all that remains to be established is whether the engine burst into flames when its captors attempted to restart it, or was a smoke flare strategically placed beneath it to make a good propaganda picture?

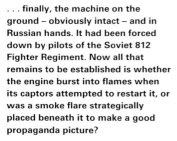

A scene of tranquility, giving little hint that the greatest tank battle in military history is just about to erupt. These machines of I./JG 52 were photographed in the midday sun on a lush meadow outside the village of Bessonovka, east of Byelgorod, which was to be their base during the opening rounds of Operation *Zitadelle*

At the beginning of July *Stab*, I. and III./JG 52 were transferred from the Kuban up into the Ukraine. The reason for the move was the imminent launch of Hitler's third annual eastern front offensive. But *Zitadelle* was no massive undertaking along the lines of the previous years' *Barbarossa* or *Blau*. It encompassed little more than 125 miles (200 km) of front from north to south. Nor were its aims as grandiose. The intention was to eliminate the bulge which had developed to the west of Kursk (recaptured by the Red Army in February) and destroy the enemy forces massing within its perimeter.

Although *Zitadelle* may have been limited in scope, the enormous build-up of armour by both sides resulted in its developing into the largest tank battle in military history. As such, the dominant aerial role in the Battle of Kursk was played by the Luftwaffe's specialised ground-attack units (see *Osprey Aviation Elite Units 13 - Luftwaffe Schlachtgruppen* for further details). The main task of the eight *Jagdgruppen* involved in *Zitadelle* was to protect their own Panzer divisions from the deadly Il-2s.

On 5 July, the opening day of the offensive, Luftwaffe fighters claimed no fewer than 432 enemy aircraft destroyed. In terms of numbers of machines shot down, it was the greatest single day of aerial combat of the entire war. JG 52's contribution to this total was headed by Hauptmann Johannes Wiese, the acting *Kommandeur* of I. *Gruppe*, who added a round dozen to his personal tally. 7./JG 52's Oberleutnant Walter Krupinski came a close second, his 11 victories bringing his own score to 90, and helping his *Staffel* achieve its collective 750.

Forty-eight hours later, a kill by 2. *Staffel's* Oberleutnant Paul-Heinrich Dähne (who would lose his own life in a He 162 *Volksjäger* jet just two weeks before the end of the war) was notable on two counts – it took I. *Gruppe's* score to 800, and the *Geschwader's* overall total to 6000. 7 May was of some significance for 'Bubi' Hartmann too. Not only was it his most successful day to date – with four La-5s and a trio of *Sturmoviks* downed – it also offered him his first taste of command. With his close friend and guiding light Walter Krupinski wounded, the 21-year-old Hartmann took over as acting-*Kapitän* of 7. *Staffel*.

Despite continuing success in the air, the situation on the ground was not looking good. German forces attacking from both north and south

The Battle of Kursk was at its height when Hauptmann Johannes Wiese, the acting *Kommandeur* of I./JG 52, achieved his century

had failed to link up and 'pinch off' the Kursk salient. Worse, on 11 July the Red Army mounted a strong counter-offensive towards Orel behind the eight divisions of the northern attack force which threatened to isolate them. Unnerved by this move, and needing to transfer some of his eastern front ground units to the new danger zone of the Mediterranean (where Anglo-American forces had invaded Sicily on 10 July), Hitler ordered the abandonment of *Zitadelle* on 13 July. The Führer's last great gamble in the east had failed. For the Red Army, the road to Berlin lay ahead.

In the immediate aftermath of Kursk, III. *Gruppe* was sent up to Orel to help contain the Soviet threat to that area, while I./JG 52 retired to Poltava. With the enemy beginning to push and probe at all points along the overstretched southern sector, these were but the first of more than a dozen moves each *Gruppe* would make over the course of the next two months as they were 'shuffled about like demented chess pieces'.

Although JG 52 had suffered a further 29 casualties in July – well over a third of its current operational strength – individual scores continued to

Not to be outdone in the floral department, 5./JG 52 awarded future Knight's Cross recipient Leutnant Peter 'Bonifaz' Düttmann a huge garland of sunflowers when he claimed the *Staffel's* 500th victory on 25 July 1943

An exception to the rule that all 'black men' be nameless was Erich Hartmann's crew chief, and great personal friend, Heinz 'Bimmel' Mertens. Such was the bond between these two that when his pilot failed to return from an early morning sortie on 20 August 1943, Mertens armed himself with a rifle and set off on his own behind enemy lines to search for him!

grow. On 2 August *Kommodore* Hrabak reached his century. The following day the last of a quartet of Soviet fighters took Erich Hartmann to 50. In little more than a fortnight that figure would nearly double to 90. But number 90 – the second of a pair of Il-2s downed in the early morning of 20 August – very nearly changed the course of aviation history.

In almost a re-run of his first kill, pieces from the doomed *Sturmovik*, which was ablaze from nose to tail, smashed into the undersides of Hartmann's fighter as he pulled up hard above it. Again, his cockpit rapidly filling with smoke, he had no choice but to crash-land as quickly as possible. But this time he was *behind* enemy lines. It was only by feigning injury that Hartmann managed to escape from his captors and return on foot the following day. That moment's laxity by two Russian guards was to cost the Red Air Force another 255 frontline aircraft!

By the latter half of August Soviet pressure on the Ukraine was increasing steadily. To the north, Kharkov was finally retaken on 23 August. Six days later, in the south, Taganrog was liberated, and the Red Army began its advance along the shores of the Sea of Azov. Between the

two (in both time and place) there was a brief spell when all three *Gruppen* – II./JG 52 having been recently withdrawn from the Kuban after nearly five months in support of 17. *Armee* – shared a large field to the east of Stalino. But all too soon operational requirements dictated that each went its separate way again.

On 29 August Hauptmann Günther Rall, who had assumed command of III. *Gruppe* on the second day of *Zitadelle,* became the third pilot to achieve a double century (the Swords would follow on 12 September). On the debit side, Leutnant Berthold Korts was posted missing in the

Another example of the close links forged between pilot and groundcrew was provided by Hauptmann Günther Rall on the occasion of his double century, claimed at Makeyevka on 29 August. As well as posing with fellow pilots for a commemorative snapshot (also see page 71 of *Osprey Aircraft of the Aces 37 - Bf 109 Aces of the Russian Front*), Rall – third from left – made sure that his mechanics were part of the celebrations too

Much more formal attire a fortnight later, though, when Hauptmann Rall attended a small awards ceremony at the Führer's *Wolfsschanze* (Wolf's lair) HQ, in East Prussia, to receive the Swords. The full line-up, from left, is comprised of Major Hartmann Grasser (ex-JG 51), Hauptmann Heinrich *Prinz* zu Sayn-Wittgenstein (NJG 3), Rall and Oberleutnant Walter Nowotny (JG 54)

97

Kharkov area. Korts had been leading the *'Karaya' Staffel* since the loss of Ernst Ehrenberg back in May. His total was standing at 113 when notification of the award of his Knight's Cross was received at Makeyevka – on the very day he disappeared. Korts' replacement as *Staffelkapitän* of 9./JG 52 was Leutnant Erich Hartmann, who was to become the most famous *'Karaya-Eins'* of them all.

Two other changes of command occurred in the first week of September. Hauptmann Gerhard Barkhorn took over II. *Gruppe* from the departing Helmut Kühle. And when Oberleutnant Heinz 'Johnny' Schmidt failed to return from a mission on 5 September (it was reported that he had been shot down in error by a Hungarian fighter), he was replaced at the head of 6. *Staffel* by the up-and-coming Leutnant Helmut Lipfert.

By this time the German evacuation of the entire Donetz basin was well under way. JG 52's pilots were not sorry to say goodbye to the area's soggy forward landing grounds, their surface churned to mud by the early autumn rains. But they did not have long to enjoy the benefits of the paved runways of the airfields further to the rear around Poltava and Kiev before finding themselves on the move again.

The Führer had finally agreed to 17. *Armee's* abandoning its last toehold in the Kuban. On the night of 15 September the first of the nearly quarter-of a-million men packed into the Taman peninsula began crossing the Straits of Kerch on to the Crimea. The following day Hauptmann Johannes Wiese's I. *Gruppe* flew in to Taman airfield to help cover their withdrawal.

The evacuation would last until 9 October, and throughout much of this time (at first from Taman, but latterly – reinforced by 6. *Staffel* – from Kerch IV, on the Crimean side of the straits) I./JG 52 continued to offer support. In addition to protecting the ground troops and evacuation vessels from air attack, it also provided a continual relay of fighter escorts for the vulnerable *Mausis* (minesweeping Ju 52/3ms) struggling to keep the three-mile-wide straits free of Soviet mines. By the time the campaign in the Kuban was finally over, it was estimated that the Red Air Force had lost in excess of 2250 aircraft.

On 1 September 1943 Hauptmann Gerhard Barkhorn took command of II./JG 52. He would lead the *Gruppe* until January 1945. Note the *Gustav* in the background, its *Kommandeur* chevrons embellished by Barkhorn's personal 'lucky 5'

1. *Staffel's* 'White 10' undergoes some essential maintenance in the field. The date of this shot has been given as September 1943, but the location has not been established. The featureless expanse of surrounding grassland offers no clue, and could be almost any one of the nine different fields occupied by I./JG 52 during the course of this one month alone (although this number is reduced to just six if, as one source suggests, 'White 10' was lost on 14 September)

Pictured here a year earlier as a leutnant wearing the Oak Leaves awarded for his century, the eventful career of Heinz 'Johnny' Schmidt – which included six days behind enemy lines on one occasion, and a two-day trek across the frozen Sea of Azov minus one fur-lined flying boot and with a smashed shoulder on another – was brought tragically to an end when he was reportedly shot down in error by a Hungarian fighter

'The most famous *Karaya-Eins* of them all'. Leutnant Erich Hartmann, the *Staffelkapitän* of 9./JG 52, with his 'Yellow 1'. The G-6's rudder displays a total of 121 kills – the 121st being a La-5, which was the last of four victories all claimed on 2 October close to III./JG 52's Novo-Zaporozhe base

Meanwhile, the Russian advance across the northern Ukraine was gaining momentum as German forces fell back on the Dnieper, leaving a trail of scorched earth behind them. On 23 September, three days after Erich Hartmann claimed his century, the Soviets retook Polatva. Soon Kiev, the Ukrainian capital, would be liberated, and once across the Dnieper there were no more major barriers between the Red Army and the Polish border.

But it was to the south, in the steppe between the lower reaches of the Dnieper and the Sea of Azov, that the more immediate danger threatened. Here, the Soviets were driving hard for the Perekop isthmus, aiming to sever all landward connections to the Crimea. This they achieved on 30 October. For 17. *Armee*, so recently escaped from the Kuban, it was a case of out of the frying pan into the fire. They were now completely cut off again.

The High Command immediately began to draw up plans for the evacuation by sea of all forces on the Crimea. But Hitler would have none of it. The Führer's mind was still focused on oil – although by now not of the Caucasian variety, but Rumanian. If the Crimea were to be abandoned, it would provide a host of airfields from which the Red Air Force could launch bombing raids on the vital Rumanian oilfields that surrounded Ploesti. And so the order was given. Like the Kuban before it, the Crimea was to be 'held at all costs'. Despite being well below half strength, JG 52 was about to renew its long-standing relationship with 17. *Armee*.

Leaving III. *Gruppe* on the Dnieper, where Erich Hartmann was awarded the Knight's Cross – for 148 kills – on 29 October, *Stab*, I. and II./JG 52 flew into the beleaguered Crimea before the month was out. By this time the peninsula was coming under attack from three sides. While Soviet units were battering their way down the Perekop isthmus into the northern Crimea, another force had followed the retreating 17. *Armee* across the Straits of Kerch and established a bridgehead on its easternmost tip. And along the coastline to the northeast, yet more troops were infiltrating the marshy flatlands edging the inland Sivash (or 'Putrid') Sea.

Although the pressure on the Crimea was intense, a renewed Russian offensive to the west of the Dnieper, which was threatening to split Army Group South in two, had the makings of an even greater catastrophe. This resulted in Hauptmann Wiese's 'fire brigade' I. *Gruppe* being rushed northwards on 20 November to join the now Major Günther Rall's III./JG 52 in the Kirovograd area. And with the *Geschwaderstab* having withdrawn to Nikolayev three days earlier, only II. *Gruppe* now remained in support of 17. *Armee*.

These were JG 52's dispositions as the year approached its end. But whether helping to shore up the crumbling Ukraininan front between the Dnieper and Bug rivers, or taking part in the defence of the Crimea, the *Geschwader's* pilots were still making the enemy pay dearly for every metre of soil liberated.

On 29 November *Kommodore* Oberstleutnant Dietrich Hrabak was awarded the Oak Leaves for 118 victories. But it was JG 52's 'top trio' of Rall, Barkhorn and Hartmann who were now clearly emerging from the

As the German retreat gathered momentum, JG 52's bases were subjected to ever more frequent air attacks. Silhouetted by the setting sun at their backs, two members of I. *Gruppe's* ground staff scan the darkening eastern horizon for the first signs of a dusk raid, while a pilot keeps watch from the cockpit of his *Gustav*

An all too familiar scene – clouds of smoke shroud a forward landing ground as another *Sturmovik* bores in low to add its load to the devastation already caused

It was the accepted custom in the *Jagdwaffe* that returning pilots were greeted first by their crew chiefs. Here, Major Günther Rall gets a hearty handshake for victory number 250 (a La-5 brought down south of Zaporozhe on 28 November). Only after this ritual had been observed could his fellow pilots carry Rall, shoulder-high, glass in hand, to the mess tent, where further refreshment awaited

ranks, and who would dominate this closing chapter of the unit's history. On 28 November Major Günther Rall became only the second Luftwaffe fighter pilot to reach 250. Forty-eight hours later Hauptmann Gerhard Barkhorn was the fifth to achieve a double century. Closing fast on the two veterans, Oberleutnant Erich Hartmann was credited with his 150th on 13 December.

Collectively, JG 52 had become the first *Jagdgeschwader* to claim 8000 enemy aircraft destroyed with the downing of an Il-2 on 4 December. Exactly four months earlier, another of the seemingly ever-present *Sturmoviks* had ended the operational career of 4. *Staffel's* Fahnenjunker-Feldwebel Werner Quast. Rammed by his heavily armoured opponent over the Soviet-held Black Sea coast, 'Quax' Quast had baled out and been taken prisoner. He received the last of 1943's eight Knight's Crosses, awarded to him *in absentia* on 31 December.

The events of the first week of 1944 did not bode well for the future. Yet another new Soviet offensive to the west of the Dnieper was aimed at driving a wedge between Army Groups South and Centre. The important town of Zhitomir, 75 miles (120 km) west of Kiev, had been freed on 1 January. Eight days later the Red Army entered Kirovograd.

Based at the oddly named Malaja-Wiska (inevitably 'Malaya-Whiskey' to the troops), which was situated only 25 miles (40 km) west-northwest of Kirovograd, I. and III. *Gruppen* had their closest shave yet. Before dawn on 9 January, Soviet tanks, supported by infantry, penetrated onto the airfield. In the ensuing firefight, groundcrews of both *Gruppen* suffered casualties and a lot of equipment, including the ops room signals centre, was destroyed.

At first light a *Gruppe* of ground-attack Fw 190s, which had remained unscathed on the far side of the large airfield, took to the air and – with the help of the base's own flak defences – managed to repulse the attackers. Daylight revealed the extent of the destruction. III./JG 52's dispersal area had been hardest hit. Major Rall's *Gruppe*, which had lost just two machines in action over the past two months, reported that seven *Gustavs* and the unit's Klemm Kl 35 runabout had been severely damaged. Most had been rammed by the careening Russian tanks.

The confused nature of the ground fighting in the Ukraine during the next two months was reflected in the many complicated moves forced upon I. and III./JG 52 as separate *Staffeln*, and even individual *Schwärme*, were hived off to deal with myriad local crises. Nor again was the Red Army the only enemy to contend with. Although the winter of 1943-44 had not been too severe in the south, the early spring thaws posed serious problems. The thick mud immobilised fuel bowsers, resulting in 45-gallon (200 l) fuel drums having to be loaded onto horse-drawn carts and taken out to the machines for refuelling by hand. And the glutinous spray

When Hauptmann Gerhard Barkhorn claimed his 250th kill over the Crimea on 13 February 1944, his crew chief handed him a glass and toasted his success even before he clambered out of the cockpit. The normally reserved Barkhorn allows himself a rare smile as he surveys the elaborate placard that the groundcrew had ready and waiting

churned up by aircraft taking off clogged up radiators and quickly caused engines to overheat. Many missions were aborted as pilots turned back with temperature gauges in the red and engines in danger of seizing up altogether.

February was topped and tailed by a pair of Knight's Crosses. One went to Leutnant Hans 'Dackel' Waldmann for 84 victories and the other to Oberfeldwebel Victor Petermann for 60. Both would subsequently convert onto the Me 262 jet and join JG 7, the latter despite having lost his left arm to anti-aircraft fire and flying his final eastern front sorties – during which time he gained a further four kills – with an artificial limb.

The month also marked a further stage in the rise of Gerhard Barkhorn and Erich Hartmann. On 13 February II. *Gruppe's Kommandeur* became the third pilot to achieve 250 victories. A fortnight later ten kills in a single day near Kirovograd took 'Bubi' Hartmann past his double century to 202. The pair were honoured with two of the four decorations awarded to JG 52 on 2 March. Hauptmann Barkhorn received the Swords, while Oak Leaves were conferred upon Erich Hartmann, Oberleutnant Walter Krupinski (177 kills) and Hauptmann Johannes Wiese (125).

But personal successes and astronomical individual scores could not alter the course of the war. The strength of the Red Army and Air Force was by now overwhelming. On 4 March the Soviets launched their major spring offensive, which was to tear the southern sector apart. Responding to the frantic manoeuvring of the embattled ground forces, I. and III. *Gruppen's* combat units changed bases no fewer than 15 times during this one month alone.

Despite this, losses remained within bounds. But among the dozen March casualties was Knight's Cross holder Leutnant Hans Dammers of the *'Karaya' Staffel.* On 13 March, when his score was standing at 113, Dammers' fighter was rammed by a crashing Soviet machine. Although he managed to bale out, his parachute became entangled with the *Gustav's* tailplane. Hans Dammers died four days later of the injuries he had sustained.

Gustavs of Hauptmann Johannes Wiese's I./JG 52 are seen at dispersal on an unidentified airstrip in the southern Ukraine shortly before the Red Army's major 1944 spring offensive that was to drive the *Gruppe* back into Rumania

Leutnant Hans Dammers of 9./JG 52, whose machine was rammed by a crashing Soviet fighter on 13 March, was photographed as an oberfeldwebel at Byelgorod in May 1943 on the occasion of his century – note the '100' at the bottom of the rudder, partially obscured by his signature. For an illustration of the starboard side of this rudder, on which Dammers kept a meticulous record of all his ground-attack successes, see page 74 of *Osprey Aircraft of the Aces 37 - Bf 109 Aces of the Russian Front*

Awarded the Knight's Cross on 26 March for 100+ victories (he had achieved his century over three months earlier), Leutnant Otto Fönnekold is shown here astride a Zündapp KS750 heavy motorcycle combination, with an unidentified fellow II. *Gruppe* pilot on the pillion. Although JG 52's aircraft no longer carried Major Trübenach's 'winged sword' *Geschwader* emblem, note its retention on the front of the sidecar

On the other side of the coin, JG 52 continued to inflict serious damage on the enemy. Major Rall's III. *Gruppe* had consolidated its lead, claiming an overall 3500 enemy aircraft destroyed by 21 March 1944. During the following week another clutch of Knight's Crosses was awarded. Three went to *Staffelkapitäne* for scores ranging from 75 to 82 (see Appendix 2). The fourth was presented to II. *Gruppe's* Leutnant Otto Fönnekold, an ex-NCO who had already been commissioned in the field for 'bravery in action', and who had passed the 100 mark back in January.

The *Geschwader* garnered three more Knight's Crosses in the first week of April. Again, two were awarded to *Staffelkapitäne* (for 90 and 74 victories, respectively), while the last was a posthumous honour for 7./JG 52's Leutnant Johann Bunzek, who had been killed when his machine exploded in mid-air after colliding with a Soviet fighter over Nikopol on 11 December 1943. At the time of his loss, Bunzek had been credited with 75 Soviet aircraft shot down, plus another 30 unconfirmed.

While I. and III./JG 52 helped shore up the crumbling Ukrainian front, Hauptmann Barkhorn's II. *Gruppe* had been supporting the isolated 17. *Armee* in its dogged defence of the Crimea. But since II./JG 52's arrival at Bagerovo, close to the Straits of Kerch, at the end of October, unremitting Soviet pressure from both east and north had forced the Germans back across almost the entire width of the peninsula. By the second week of April, the situation was becoming desperate as the defenders were compressed ever more tightly into the south-western tip of the Crimea, around the historic battlefields of Sevastopol and Balaclava.

Barkhorn's pilots were pushing themselves to the limit in their efforts to protect the ground troops, but they badly needed reinforcement themselves. It was to be provided by III. *Gruppe*, which – after exactly four days back in Rumania spent guarding the Ploesti oil wells – flew in to the airfield complex on Cape Khersonyes, immediately to the south of Sevastopol, on 10 April. II./JG 52 joined them there four days later for the final act in the Crimean drama.

During the next month, despite near constant attacks on the cape's three main landing rounds by Red Air Force bombers and *Sturmoviks,* the *Gruppens'* pilots each flew on average five sorties a day. In addition to normal fighter sweeps, their missions included escorting their own

On 18 April 1944 Major Günther Rall bade farewell to III./JG 52, the *Gruppe* he had served with since 1940, and which he had commanded for the past nine months. This informal shot shows him – second from left, wearing an inflatable lifejacket – with a group of his NCO pilots on an airfield 'somewhere in the east'. Here, too, the *Gruppe* emblem, removed from the unit's fighters for security reasons, is still on prominent display on the ground

ground-assault units, protecting the supply vessels running the gauntlet across the Black Sea from Rumania (the Russian port of Odessa had been recaptured by the Red Army on 10 April), providing battlefield reconnaissance and ground strafing. Faced with this multiplicity of tasks, II. *Gruppe* was still managing to bring down nearly two-dozen enemy aircraft every day. For the month of April Luftwaffe fighters claimed a total of 1010 Soviet aircraft destroyed over and around the Crimea.

It was in the midst of all this action that the *Geschwader* said goodbye to one of its stalwarts. On 18 April Major Günther Rall, his score standing at 273, was posted back to the Reich to take command of II./JG 11. Rall's appointed successor at the head of III. *Gruppe* was recent centurion Hauptmann Wilhelm Batz, the ex-*Staffelkapitän* of 5./JG 52. But as Batz was not yet recovered from wounds suffered four days earlier, III./JG 52 would be led by acting-*Kommandeur* Oberleutnant Erich Hartmann until 28 May.

With the departure of several of JG 52's 'old guard' (Walter Krupinski was another who had been recalled for defence of the Reich duties), a number of the younger names began to fill positions of command. In April Gerhard Barkhorn welcomed two new *Staffelkapitäne* – 'Dackel' Waldmann took over 4./JG 52, while Otto Fönnekold replaced Wilhelm Batz at the head of 5. *Staffel*.

By now the end in the Crimea was in sight. On 7 May the Red Air Force carried out six heavy raids on II. and III. *Gruppens'* bases at Khersonyes. 6./JG 52 was particularly badly hit, and when *Staffelkapitän* Oberleutnant Helmut Lipfert tried to take off in the unit's last serviceable fighter 48 hours later, the *Gustav* was damaged by artillery fire and he had to abort. Lipfert, who had claimed his century over the Crimea on 11 April, was forced to vacate the peninsula stuffed into the rear fuselage of the *Gruppen*-Adjutant's machine!

The evacuation proper had begun on 8 May. Over the next four days some 150,000 men of 17. *Armee* staged their own 'mini-Dunkirk', escaping across the Black Sea to Rumania in a flotilla of small ships. But like the BEF before them, they had had to leave behind all their vehicles and heavy equipment.

Although he had been with the *Gruppe* for little more than two years, Oberleutnant Walter Krupinski, *Kapitän* of 7. *Staffel*, was another of III./JG 52's mainstays. On 2 March he had been awarded the Oak Leaves to add to his Knight's Cross won back in October 1942 (and which he is seen wearing here as a leutnant). Like *Kommandeur* Günther Rall, Krupinski – or *'Graf Punski'* (Count Punski), as he was known to one and all – was also posted back to Germany to join a Defence of the Reich *Geschwader*. He ended the war flying Me 262s with JV 44

Rumania was also the destination of acting-*Kommandeur* Erich Hartmann's III./JG 52, each pilot removing his machine's radio and armour in order to be able to accommodate *two* members of the ground staff for the 200-mile (330 km) flight across the Black Sea. But it was II. *Gruppe* which received that week's two Knight's Crosses. 5. *Staffel's* Leutnant Peter 'Bonifaz' Düttmann, who had claimed nine kills on 7 May – the day of the heavy Soviet raids on Khersonyes – was decorated 48 hours later for a total of 91 victories. And on 14 May Fahnenjunker-Feldwebel Gerhard 'Fakken' Hoffmann of 4./JG 52 was awarded his for a score of 125.

Although on widely dispersed airfields, the reuniting of JG 52 in Rumania (*Stab* and I. *Gruppe* would fly in from the German-held rump of the southwest Ukraine in June) meant that the *Geschwader's* eastern front odyssey had come full circle. The pilots were back where they had started from three years earlier. But in those three years the inadequately-led, obsolescent Red Air Force of 1941 had grown into a powerful, well-equipped colossus which outnumbered the Luftwaffe in Rumania by some forty to one.

And now there was another enemy. Since early April, the vital oil wells around Ploesti had been attracting the attention of increasing numbers of US heavy bombers of the Fifteenth Air Force, based in Italy. JG 52 thus found itself facing an entirely new kind of opponent when sent up against the American formations attacking the oilfields, and other targets, in Rumania. More accustomed to tackling individual, small gaggles of low-flying *Sturmoviks*, the high-altitude boxes of US heavy bombers, comprising anything from 100 to 600 machines, came as a rude shock to Hrabak's pilots.

Pictured standing in front of the same 'Black 12' in which he had claimed 5. *Staffel's* 500th victory (see photo on page 95), Leutnant Peter Düttmann received the Knight's Cross on 9 May for 91 kills. His final end-of-war total was 152, achieved over a two-year operational career in which he himself had been forced to bale out or crash-land no fewer than 19 times!

Another of the high scorers among the *Geschwader's* younger *Nachwuchs*, or second-generation, pilots was Oberleutnant Walter Wolfrum. Joining 5. *Staffel* in January 1943, he regularly flew this 'Black 15', which he christened *Quex*. In July 1944, two months after being appointed *Kapitän* of 1. *Staffel*, he was severely wounded. Despite then being off ops for over six months, Wolfrum ended the war with 137 confirmed victories . . .

. . . but it was one of Wolfrum's veteran NCOs, old hand Oberfeldwebel Karl Munz – nicknamed *'Fuchs'* ('Fox') by his fellow pilots – who, on 1 June 1944, was to be credited with I./JG 52's 2000th enemy aircraft destroyed

During June those missions directed specifically against the Fifteenth Air Force, which were code-named *Sternflüge* (Starflights), proved both costly and unrewarding. Unable to penetrate the strong fighter screen protecting the heavies, JG 52 claimed just three bombers. Its dozen other kills were reportedly made up of escorting P-51s and P-38s.

But it was the Red Air Force which was, and would remain, the principal enemy right up until the very end. On 30 May Hauptmann Wilhelm Batz had celebrated his return to operations at the head of III./JG 52 in Roman, northern Rumania, by claiming 15 Soviet machines in seven sorties. At nearby Jassy, Leutnant Walter Wolfrum, the *Staffelkapitän* of 1./JG 52, had downed 11, and would reach his century two days later. On that same 1 June, Oberfeldwebel Karl Munz, also of 1. *Staffel*, would be credited with I./JG 52's collective 2000th kill.

Dangerous as the situation on the eastern front undoubtedly was, the Luftwaffe High Command clearly regarded the threat posed by the US daylight bomber offensive against Germany itself as even more important – or perhaps just nearer to home? For it was at this juncture that each of JG 52's three *Gruppen* was denuded of an entire *Staffel* which was to be transferred *en bloc* to Defence of the Reich duties. Oberleutnant Paul-Heinrich Dähne's 2./JG 52 was the first to depart. Early in June, they left Jassy for Reinsehlen, where they converted to the Fw 190 for future service as 12./JG 11. By a quirk of fate, the end of the month would see them back briefly in the east, III./JG 11 having been rushed to the central sector as part of the desperate attempt to halt the great Soviet summer offensive.

4. and 7./JG 52's pilots took a different route. Both retained their Bf 109s, but before officially becoming part of the Defence of the Reich organisation – as 8. and 12. *Staffeln* of II. and III./JG 3 respectively – they would find themselves embroiled, along with their new *Gruppen*, in the latter stages of the Normandy campaign.

Meanwhile, the now six *Staffel*-strong JG 52 was getting on with its war in the east. On 18 June Gerhard Barkhorn's II. *Gruppe* had moved in to Zilistea, less than 50 miles (80 km) northwest of Ploesti. Six days later, nine of its *Gustavs* took off to intercept an incoming force of 135 B-24s, plus a strong fighter escort, in one of JG 52's last, and most successful, Starflight operations.

After twice failing to get through the fighter screen, Oberleutnant Helmut Lipfert, *Staffelkapitän* of 6./JG 52, caught a B-24 on his third

Having previously been a leading member of the RAD (Reich Labour Service), Helmut Lipfert was also a relative latecomer to the *Geschwader*. He scored his first kill with II./JG 52 on 30 January 1943. Lipfert's final total of 203 included two US heavy bombers

pass, setting its port outer engine on fire. Shortly afterwards the Liberator blew up. It was kill number 128 for Lipfert. Another of the B-24s was credited to his wingman, Unteroffizier Heinrich Tamen. Altogether, the oilfields' aerial defences (which also included elements of I. *Gruppe* and the Fw 190-equipped SG 2) claimed the destruction of nine US aircraft. But I./JG 52 had lost four of its own pilots – two killed and two wounded – and was now reduced to just seven serviceable machines.

The Fifteenth Air Force would continue to batter Ploesti until August. But the massive Soviet summer offensive – unleashed against Army Group Centre on 22 June, the third anniversary of *Barbarossa* – meant that JG 52 was urgently required elsewhere. Early July thus saw I. and II. *Gruppen* based around Lemberg (Lvov), in southern Poland, while III./JG 52 was further to the north, and just beyond the Polish border, at Minsk – the western terminus of the Moscow highway, and an old stamping ground of the *Geschwader's* veteran members.

Although they could do nothing to halt the Soviet juggernaut bearing down on them (Minsk was recaptured by the Red Army on 3 July), the pilots of JG 52 were still making the enemy pay a heavy price. On 4 July Erich Hartmann received the Swords for 239 victories. By the time of the award, however, that total was already well out of date. Some sources state that four Yak fighters and a trio of *Sturmoviks* downed near Bobruisk four days previously had taken his total to exactly 250.

Hartmann was the fourth of only five pilots to reach this figure. And it provides an illuminating view of the relative values officially placed upon 'eastern' versus 'western' scores to compare his achievement with that of

Oberstleutnant Josef Priller, *Kommodore* of JG 26 in the west, who had also been honoured with the Swords just 48 hours earlier – for his century!

Against the mass of the Red Air Force, scores of 100 or more, while not exactly the norm, were no longer regarded as unusual. During June and July five more members of JG 52 were awarded the Knight's Cross for totals either nearing, or already surpassing, the century. And this against a background of continual transfers, not just from one airfield to another, but now from one country to another. Towards the end of this period, as the huge Red Army offensive gathered ever more momentum, elements of the *Geschwader* were shuttled from Poland up into Lithuania, back into Poland and then down to Hungary and Rumania!

As always, however, the successes were offset by losses. On 16 July ten of the 28 kills claimed by I. *Gruppe* near Kamionka, northeast of Lemberg, were credited to Leutnant Walter Wolfrum. But after the tenth, the *Kapitän* of 1. *Staffel* was himself hit and so severely wounded that he would be off ops until February 1945.

On 20 July Hauptmann Wilhelm Batz was awarded the Oak Leaves for 175 victories. Four days later fellow *Gruppenkommandeur* Hauptmann Adolf Borchers, who had arrived from JG 51 on 11 June to take over from Johannes Wiese at the head of I./JG 52, reached his 100.

On 27 July Leutnant Hans-Joachim Birkner, who had often flown as wingman to Günther Rall and Erich Hartmann, received the Knight's Cross for 98 kills – a total he had amassed in less than ten months. Another of 27 July's three Knight's Cross recipients, Leutnant Herbert Bachnick of 9. *Staffel*, would be killed in a forced landing after damage suffered attacking a formation of Eighth Air Force B-17s over Poland on 7 August. These bombers were part of the second shuttle mission to the USSR, and were temporarily based at Mirgorod, in the recently liberated Ukraine.

But any account of JG 52's later months must inevitably return to the most famous and successful 'second-generationer' of them all – Erich Hartmann. Seen here wearing the Swords won on 4 July 1944, Oberleutnant Hartmann briefs a young unteroffizier in preparation for their next mission together. Although his personal score was now rapidly approaching the 300 mark, 'Bubi' Hartmann perhaps took even more pride in the fact that he had never lost a wingman in combat

I. *Gruppe*, which had been stationed at Cracow, in Poland, alongside III./JG 52 since 1 August, was the first to be brought back up to full three-*Staffel* strength when a new 2./JG 52 was activated on 15 August under Oberleutnant Rudolf Trenkel. Barely 24 hours later it lost all its fighters when the unit was instructed to hand them over to JG 51, which had been suffering heavy attrition up in East Prussia on the northern flank of the Russian offensive.

Then action flared up again in the south with the Red Army's invasion of Rumania on 20 August. Three days later Hitler's erstwhile ally, Marshal Ion Antonescu, was overthrown and imprisoned. And 48 hours after that the new regime declared war on Germany.

II./JG 52 pilots and groundcrews, who had been ordered down into Rumania on 21 August to help the local ground forces, now found themselves in danger of being cut off and taken prisoner. Based at Bacau with 19 serviceable *Gustavs*, but only 12 pilots, Hauptmann Lipfert – acting-*Kommandeur* in the absence of Gerhard Barkhorn, who was still recovering from wounds received during one of June's Starflights – had to think fast. Ordering his fighters to scramble, he used ten of them to escort the unit's two Ju 52/3m transports westwards across the Carpathian Mountains to Sächsisch-Regen (Reghin), while the remaining pair supported the troops defending Bacau from the now hostile Rumanians.

Upon arriving at Sächsisch-Regen, Helmut Lipfert quickly organised a band of volunteer pilots from a Bf 109-equipped reconnaissance *Staffel*, who then boarded one of the Ju 52/3ms for the 110-mile (180-km) return flight back across the enemy-held Carpathians to Bacau. Here, despite coming under constant heavy fire, the reconnaissance pilots got all seven waiting *Gustavs* safely into the air, after which the Ju 52/3m successfully evacuated the last of the ground personnel.

Sadly, all this effort was to go to waste, for on 31 August – two days after II. *Gruppe* had arrived at Sächsisch-Regen – the field was strafed by a group of Fifteenth Air Force Mustangs. Used as a main collecting point for Luftwaffe units retreating from the Soviets, the base was crowded with aircraft of all types. Some 60 machines were destroyed on the ground, 29 of them fighters. A further nine were downed in aerial combat. This time it was II./JG 52's turn to be reduced to just seven serviceable machines.

While II. *Gruppe* was caught up in the defection of Rumania, there had been growing excitement among the members of III./JG 52 now stationed to the south of Warsaw. On 17 August *Kommandeur* Wilhelm Batz had reached his 200. But everybody's attention was focused on 'Bubi' Hartmann's rapidly approaching triple century – an unprecedented figure in the history of aerial warfare!

Having overtaken Gerhard Barkhorn, Erich Hartmann was nearing his 300 in leaps and bounds. On 22 August five Soviet fighters claimed in two sorties had taken him to 282. The following day another eight enemy machines made it 290 – just ten to go!

On the morning of 24 August the weather looked unpromising. It did not begin to clear up until nearly noon. Immediately after lunch, the leader of the *'Karaya' Staffel* took off, with his wingman tucked in beside him. Exactly one hour later the pair returned. Six times the distinctively marked, black-nosed *Gustav* roared low across the forward landing field rocking its wings – six down, four to go!

This shot purportedly shows Erich Hartmann buzzing the forward landing ground at Warzyn, south of Warsaw, on 24 August upon his return from the sortie which made him a triple centurion (note 9. *Staffel's* 'pierced heart' standard, which also features miniatures of III. *Gruppe's* 'barbed cross' and the *Geschwader's* 'winged sword' in the top left- and right-hand corners respectively) . . .

To the crowd gathered around 9. *Staffel's* dispersal area, refuelling and rearming the two fighters seemed to take forever. But at last they were off again. Warned by ground control of an approaching band of Airacobras, the two Bf 109s positioned themselves for the attack. Covered by his wingman, Hartmann waded in, claiming four of the lend-lease fighters in the space of just ten minutes. He had done it!

Congratulations filled the airwaves as the two Messerschmitts turned for home. Despite the hubbub over the R/T, Hartmann even found time *en route* to hack an unwary Pe-2 from a formation of light bombers to make it 301.

After the five obligatory victory passes, Hartmann landed to a tumultuous reception. The first to greet him, of course, was his chief mechanic and great friend 'Bimmel' Mertens. Then it was the turn of

. . . and this is the aircraft in which he did it. Although, in his excitement, the photographer has managed to all but decapitate its famous pilot, this picture does offer a good close-up of the markings carried by this particular *Karaya-Eins* (obviously a late model *Gustav* – note the clear-vision *Erla* canopy and lack of aerial mast) . . .

. . . lastly, and only for the perfectionist modeller, an even closer view of 9./JG 52's celebrated emblem. Rather than being stencilled, this somewhat lopsided example has clearly been painted by hand. Note the name *Ursel* – one of three which Hartmann applied to his machines at various times, the others being *Usch* and *Uschi*, all of which are accepted diminutives of Ursula, his soon-to-be wife

Kommandeur Willi Batz and the *Kommodore*, Oberstleutnant Dietrich Hrabak. War correspondents and cameramen captured the scene in words and pictures as Erich Hartmann was lifted from the cockpit of *Karaya-Eins* and carried shoulder-high through the cheering throng. A ground crewman pushed forward to place a hastily fashioned, and somewhat misshapen garland of evergreen around his neck as the celebrations began.

The next day telegrams of congratulations arrived from Hermann Göring and Adolf Hitler, the latter's also containing instructions to report to the Führer's *Wolfsschanze* HQ in East Prussia for the presentation of the Diamonds two days hence. Dr Goebbel's propaganda ministry made the most of the event, grateful for an item of good news among the dire reports flooding in from every fighting front. For with the Allies now closing in on the Reich from all sides, the war was entering its final phase.

On 31 August JG 52 was back to harsh reality when 5. *Staffel's* Oberleutnant Otto Fönnekold was shot down by marauding Mustangs as he came in to land at Budak after a mission. His loss left II. *Gruppe* with just two officer pilots – acting-*Kommandeur* Helmut Lipfert and Hauptmann Heinrich Sturm, who now took over at the head of 5./JG 52.

The *Geschwader* was soon in the news again (although not specifically identified for security reasons). On 2 September victory number 118 for Hauptmann Borchers gave JG 52 a collective total of 10,000 enemy aircraft destroyed! This achievement is all the more remarkable for the fact that the last 1000 had been scored in just under four months, during much of which time the *Geschwader* had consisted of only six *Staffeln*.

Once again the propaganda machine went into overdrive. A special '*Geschwader* March' was even composed and played on the state radio. But of far greater import to the members of JG 52 was a change of command at month's end. On 30 September the long-serving Oberstleutnant Dietrich Hrabak was appointed *Kommodore* of JG 54 (see *Osprey Aviation Elite Units 6 - Jagdgeschwader 54 'Grünherz'* for further details).

The officer who replaced him, and who would lead the *Geschwader* for the remainder of the war, was its first Diamonds winner – and erstwhile

On 30 September 1944 Oberstleutnant Dietrich Hrabak returned to his original unit – JG 54 – which he would lead until the end of the war. The *Geschwader's* longest serving *Kommodore* is pictured here a few months earlier on the occasion of a visit to JG 52 by General Otto Dessloch, GOC *Luftflotte* 4. Dessloch is the figure wearing the broad white stripes of a General Officer on his trousers. Ahead of him can be seen Major Günther Rall, with Oberstleutnant Hrabak (carrying the stick) immediately to his rear. The casual dress and demeanour – plus the Russian civilians in the background – suggest that this is very much an informal call on the General's part

Kapitän of the *'Karayas'* – Oberstleutnant Hermann Graf. JG 52 was unique in thus now having *two* Diamonds wearers within its ranks. But not even this wealth of experience and expertise could reverse the fortunes of the *Geschwader* as the Third Reich slid towards inevitable defeat.

On 1 October Erich Hartmann, who had been promoted to hauptmann exactly one month earlier bid a sad farewell to 9./JG 52. He was being transferred to II. *Gruppe*, which by now had retired into Hungary, to activate a new 4. *Staffel*.

The first Red Army troops had crossed the Hungarian border on 22 September. The country would be prevented from following Rumania's example and defecting to the Soviets by the swift intervention of German forces and the installation of a pro-Nazi government. On

The officer brought in to replace Hrabak was a very familiar name and face indeed. The arrival of the now Oberstleutnant Hermann Graf on 1 October 1944 meant that for the remaining months of the war JG 52 would be unique in having *two* Diamonds wearers within its ranks

Meanwhile, Hauptmann Erich Hartmann had been transferred to II. *Gruppe* to activate a new 4./JG 52. He took with him two essentials – the red heart of his old *'Karaya' Staffel* (albeit minus the arrow), and the even more indispensable Heinz Mertens. Wearing full 'black man's' uniform as befits the late season of the year, 'Bimmel' is seen here congratulating Erich Hartmann on his 327th victory at Budaörs, in Hungary, on 23 November 1944

10 October, the day the Russians were reported to be just 65 miles (105 km) east of the Hungarian capital Budapest, Leutnant Franz Schall was awarded the *Geschwader's* last Knight's Cross of the year for177 kills – although by the time of its announcment he had already converted to the Me 262 and was serving as a *Staffelkapitän* in the *Kommando* Nowotny.

While II. *Gruppe* would remain in Hungary until the spring of 1945, I. and III./JG 52 were already on the move again. A renewed Soviet offensive further to the north had smashed a breach between Army Groups' Centre and North. On 9 October Red Army tanks rolled across the border into East Prussia. III. *Gruppe* had already been transferred from Poland up into the Reich's north-easternmost province 24 hours earlier. I./JG 52 would follow on 16 October.

But even in defence of German soil there was little the two *Gruppen*, mustering just 40 serviceable machines between them, could do to halt the enemy's steamroller advance. Heavy Soviet artillery fire drove I. *Gruppe* from their first East Prussian field – a rudimentary landing strip near the famous stud farm of Trakehnen – within three days of their arrival. A number of *Gustavs* damaged by the incoming shells had to be hurriedly blown up before they left.

Occasionally they were able to strike back. On 21 October an armoured thrust towards Angerapp was brought to a halt by ground troops, while overhead I./JG 52 claimed ten of the attacking force's massive air umbrella. 4 November brought an unexpected visitor to I. *Gruppe's* Goldap base. A Fieseler *Storch* landed and from it clambered the unmistakeable figure of Luftwaffe Commander-in-Chief Hermann Göring. Hauptmann Borchers quickly assembled his pilots – the ground-crews were busy servicing the unit's remaining machines, ready for their next mission – who were greeted with a jovial *'Heil Flieger!'* ('Hail, flyers!') and a wave of the Reichsmarschall's jewel-encrusted baton. After a brief tour of inspection and a visit to the ops hut, the portly Göring shoehorned himself into a waiting car and was whisked off again within the hour.

On 9 November I./JG 52 returned to Cracow, in Poland. III. *Gruppe* was to stay in East Prussia for a further month.

Bad weather throughout much of November reduced air operations to a minimum. All of Hermann Graf's three widely dispersed *Gruppen* – in East Prussia, Poland and Hungary – utilised the time to acclimatise their increasingly sketchily trained, and ever younger, replacement pilots to the realities of the frontline.

The experienced members of the *Geschwader*, however ('old hares' in the Luftwaffe vernacular), were still managing to add to their scores, albeit at a greatly reduced rate. East of Budapest on 22 November (according to one reference source) the leading duo, Erich Hartmann and his *Gruppenkommandeur*, Gerhard Barkhorn, claimed numbers 322 and 283 respectively. But individual achievements in the air had no influence upon the massed movements of armies on the ground. On 8 December yet another Soviet offensive led to the encirclement of Budapest, and forced II./JG 52's retirement to Czor, northwest of the Hungarian capital, six days later.

The closing weeks of the year saw even more casualties among the *Geschwader's* formation leaders – the very people *Kommodore* Hermann Graf could least afford to lose. On 14 December Leutnant Hans-Joachim Birkner, who had taken over the *'Karaya' Staffel* from Erich Hartmann on 1 October, was killed at Cracow when his engine cut out during take-off. His final score of 117 included a solitary P-51. Another Knight's Cross-wearing *Staffelkapitän*, 5./JG 52's Hauptmann Heinrich Sturm, also lost

Staffelkapitän **Erich Hartmann confers with his new** *Gruppenkommandeur* **Major Gerhard Barkhorn – the only two fighter pilots in aviation history to achieve more than 300 kills**

his life in a take-off accident. During a scramble from Czor on 22 December, Sturm's *Gustav* somersaulted after its undercarriage clipped a truck. His career, begun as a Feldwebel with II. *Gruppe* in 1941, ended with a total of 158 victories.

And on 30 December the *Kapitän* of 8. *Staffel*, Oberleutnant Friedrich Obleser – whose Knight's Cross, like Sturm's, had been won back in March (for 80 kills) – was seriously wounded in action. Numbered among his final tally of 120 were nine American aircraft, two of them heavy bombers. Although, strictly speaking, not engaged in a two-front war, the further westward JG 52 retreated, the more often its pilots were coming into contact with the Italian-based US Fifteenth Air Force attacking targets in southeast Europe.

1945 began as 1944 had ended – with fewer victories and higher losses, all against a backdrop of unremitting Soviet pressure.

On 5 January Hauptmann Gerhard Barkhorn topped the 300 mark. Naturally, there were celebrations in honour of the Luftwaffe's second, and last, triple-centurion. But there was not the same level of propaganda hysteria as had greeted Erich Hartmann's achievement back in August. Although this was no doubt much to the relief of the quieter and more

Hauptmann Heinrich Sturm, the *Kapitän* of 5. *Staffel*, lost his life in a take-off accident at Czor, in Hungary, on 22 December 1944. He is pictured here (left) in the company of Gerhard Barkhorn (centre) and Oberleutnant Wilhelm Batz earlier in the year, when II./JG 52 was still based in the Crimea

reserved Barkhorn, there were many who thought the event at least merited a third set of Diamonds for the *Geschwader*.

A week later, the first Soviet offensive of 1945 saw the Red Army burst across Upper Silesia to the River Oder. Having retreated from Poland to the Oppeln area, southeast of Breslau, *Stab*, I. and III./JG 52 were right in the path of the enemy advance. On paper, *Kommodore* Graf's force mustered 75 serviceable fighters. But such figures are deceptive. Increasingly irregular supplies of fuel, coupled with the chaotic conditions all around, severely hampered the *Gruppen's* operations. On top of that, from the middle of January onwards, 'superfluous' members of the ground staff began to be drafted into the frontlines to serve as infantry.

On 15 January Gerhard Barkhorn was posted away to take command of JG 6. His departure led to a complete re-shuffle of JG 52's *Kommandeure* at month's end. Barkhorn's long-held position at the head of II. *Gruppe* was assumed by Hauptmann Wilhelm Batz, whose own III. *Gruppe* was then taken over by Major Adolf Borchers. Finally, the vacancy left by Borchers' move to III. *Gruppe* was filled by Hauptmann Erich Hartmann. The only member of the 'top trio' still serving with the *Geschwader*, 'Bubi' Hartmann was now the *Kommandeur* of its I. *Gruppe*.

Major Barkhorn's transfer to the command of JG 6 on 15 January 1945 resulted in one final round of command changes within JG 52. Gerhard Barkhorn's position at the head of II. *Gruppe* was taken by Hauptmann Wilhelm Batz . . .

. . . who was in turn replaced as *Kommandeur* of III./JG 52 by Major Adolf Borchers (seen here as a hauptmann). It was Borchers who had been credited with the *Geschwader's* collective 10,000th kill on 2 September 1944

Quite what these elaborate command changes were meant to achieve is not clear. The war continued – as too did the losses and the enforced retreats. At the beginning of the year Oberleutnant Heinrich Füllgrabe, an ex-member of Graf's *'Karaya' Staffel* who had followed his erstwhile *Kapitän* into the Defence of the Reich organisation, had returned to JG 52. But the eastern front was no longer as he knew it, and he did not survive for long. Hit by flak during a low-level attack on a group of Red Army tanks, Füllgrabe crashed in flames behind enemy lines on 30 January.

The continued Soviet push through Upper Silesia forced Hermann Graf's I. and III. *Gruppen* back, first to Breslau, and then southwest to Weidenguth, close to the Czechoslovakian border. But even here they were not safe from attack by waves of *Sturmoviks* and Russian-flown Douglas Boston light bombers.

On 15 February the *Geschwader* had lost another valued member when 6. *Staffel's* Hauptmann Helmut Lipfert was transferred to the command of I./JG 53. Still in Hungary, it was at this late stage that 6./JG 52 was reportedly used to create a wholly new 7. *Staffel*, which it then replaced. For the final few weeks of the war the *Geschwader* was thus back to a full nine-*Staffel* establishment.

In early March Erich Hartmann was 'invited' by General Adolf Galland to join his élite Me 262-equipped JV 44. Hartmann was not at all thrilled at the prospect but, coming from the legendary Galland, it was tantamount to an order. Fortunately, a telegram from Oberstleutnant Graf requesting Hauptmann Hartmann's return to the *Geschwader* 'as a matter of urgency', plus a direct appeal to Gordon Gollob, Galland's successor as *General der Jagdflieger* – was enough to reverse the decision. On 25 March 'Bubi' Hartmann rejoined his I. *Gruppe*, which by this time was based at Chrudim, in Czechoslovakia.

Meanwhile, a last-gasp and little known counter-offensive by six Panzer divisions having failed to stabilise the situation in Hungary, II./JG 52 had been forced right back close to the country's western border. From its base near Steinamanger (Szombathely), the unit was only some 50 miles (80 km) south of Vienna – the Red Army's next objective.

Ending nearly six months of service in Hungary, II. *Gruppe* retired across the frontier into Austria on 28 March. Although Hauptmann Batz's men were not aware of it at the time, it was to prove a very fortunate move. On 1 April II./JG 52 transferred to the airbase at Vienna-Aspern. Nine days later it lost Leutnant Friedrich Haas, *Kapitän* of 4. *Staffel*, in a dogfight over the Austrian capital. Haas managed to bale out, but at 260 ft (80 m), he was too low for his parachute to open fully.

Leutnant Haas' posthumous Knight's Cross was one of the last four major decorations to be conferred upon the *Geschwader*. All were presented in April. 3. *Staffel's* Oberleutnant Anton Resch and Leutnant Heinz 'Esau' Ewald of 5./JG 52 each received the Knight's Cross, while the final award of all, that of the Swords, went to Hauptmann Wilhelm Batz, *Kommandeur* of II. *Gruppe*, on 21 April.

Vienna had fallen to the Red Army on 13 April, by which time II./JG 52 had withdrawn further into Austria. In Czechoslovakia, Erich Hartmann had claimed kill number 350 on 17 April. The end of the war was now exactly three weeks away – and with it the end of the road for JG 52. By 8 May three final moves had taken Hauptmann Batz's

Major Borchers' move to III. *Gruppe* then led to Hauptmann Erich Hartmann's appointment as *Gruppenkommandeur* of I./JG 52. This is one of the last known wartime photographs of 'Bubi' Hartmann. It was taken at Chrudim, in Czechoslovakia, on 17 April 1945. Hartmann has just landed after claiming his 350th victory, and is facing a crowd of well-wishers and yet more garlands – much to his obvious embarrassment! But two kills more and three weeks later and it would all be over

II. *Gruppe* to Zeltweg, in southern Austria. Oberstleutnant Hermann Graf's *Stab*, together with I. and III. *Gruppen*, were congregated on an improvised airstrip at Deutsch-Brod (Nemecky Brod), some 70 miles (110 km) southeast of the Czech capital Prague.

Kommodore Graf ordered Erich Hartmann into the air one last time. His instructions – find out how close the Red Army was to Deutsch-Brod. At 0830 hrs on 8 May Hartmann took off with his wingman to search for the Soviet spearheads. He discovered them just over 40 miles (70 km) away at Brünn (Brno). A huge pall of smoke hung above the town. Flying around it, Hartmann spotted a loose gaggle of eight Yak fighters. As if putting on a display for the troops below, the Soviets were wheeling and jinking about the sky, completely oblivious to the pair of *Gustavs* closing on them from above.

Suddenly, one of the Yaks pulled up into a loop beneath Hartmann. It was the work of a moment to dive upon the unsuspecting enemy and deliver a lethal burst of fire. Victory number 352! As the Yak went tumbling down in flames, 'Bubi' Hartmann was already lining up his second victim. But then a glint of metal high in the sky caught his eye. The reflection of sun on a polished surface could mean only one thing – there were Mustangs about as well!

Not wanting to be caught between the Soviets below and the Americans above, Hartmann and his wingman sought the cover of the smoke cloud, before setting course for base.

Back at Deutsch-Brod, everybody knew that the fight was all but over. Notification of Erich Hartmann's promotion to major did little to dispel the sombre mood. Nor did the contents of a second telegram, which read;

'Graf and Hartmann both to fly to Dortmund immediately, and there surrender to British forces. Remaining personnel JG 52 to surrender to Soviet forces at Deutsch-Brod.

'Seidemann, GOC Lw.Kdo.'

It would be a great prize for the Soviets to capture the two Diamonds wearers who, between them, had accounted for over 550 machines of the Red Air Force. But somebody at *Luftwaffenkommando HQ* or above was clearly trying to protect them. It speaks volumes for the pair's character and integrity that they decided, immediately and unanimously, to ignore the order (although neither realised at the time just what it was going to cost them).

Their first duty lay with their men. And not just the men. Many members of the two *Gruppen*, especially those from the eastern provinces, now had families with them. There were also a number of refugees, who had sought the safety of a disciplined military unit amidst the chaos and confusion of Germany's collapse.

Consequently, while the pilots of Hauptmann Batz's II./JG 52 in Austria took off from Zeltweg for Munich-Neubiberg, where they surrendered to elements of the US Army Air Forces, Hermann Graf ordered that the remaining two dozen *Gustavs* of I. and III. *Gruppen* be put to the torch at Deutsch-Brod and his motley group – numbering some 2000 in all – set out for Bavaria by road. They had hardly covered half the 100-mile (160-km) journey, however, before their trucks ran into the leading Shermans of Gen Patton's Third Army.

Now they really *were* pawns – not of military manoeuvring, but of international politics. Adhering to the strict letter of the agreement between the Allies that all units fighting on the eastern front at the time of Germany's surrender were to be regarded as prisoners of the Russians, the US troops handed the group over to the Red Army.

The events that followed are not part of this story. Suffice it to say that the ways of the two Diamonds winners soon parted. Oberstleutnant Graf and Major Hartmann each dealt with Soviet captivity in his own manner. The former was released in 1950. Erich Hartmann was not returned to Germany until October 1955.

But the preceding pages have, first and foremost, been a brief history of the Luftwaffe's, and the world's, most successful fighter unit. It is therefore only proper that they should close with the statistics which allow the *Geschwader* to lay rightful claim to this title.

In round figures, German fighters were credited with some 70,000 enemy aircraft destroyed during World War 2. Approximately 45,000 of this total were amassed on the eastern front. And if one respected air historian's contention that the *Geschwader's* pilots between them accounted for close on 10,600 Soviet machines is correct, then nearly a quarter of all Red Air Force aircraft shot down by Luftwaffe fighters during World War 2 fell to JG 52!

APPENDICES

APPENDIX 1

COMMANDING OFFICERS

Kommodoren

von Bernegg, *Maj* Merhart	19/8/39	to	18/8/40
Trübenbach, *Maj* Hanns	19/8/40	to	10/10/41
Lessmann, *Maj* Wilhelm	15/10/41	to	2/6/42 (+)
Beckh, *Obstlt* Friedrich	3/6/42	to	21/6/42 (+)
Ihlefeld, *Maj* Herbert	22/6/42	to	28/10/42
Hrabak, *Obstlt* Dietrich	1/11/42	to	30/9/44
Graf, *Obstlt* Hermann	1/10/44	to	8/5/45

Gruppenkommandeure

I./JG 52

von Pfeil und Klein-Ellguth, *Hptm* Dietrich *Graf*	1/11/38	to	21/11/39
von Eschwege, *Hptm* Siegfried	1/12/39	to	26/8/40
Ewald, *Hptm* Wolfgang	27/8/40	to	24/5/41
Leesmann, *Hptm* Karl-Heinz	25/5/41	to	6/11/41
Lommel, *Oblt* Carl (acting)	6/11/41	to	?
Bennemann, *Hptm* Helmut	14/6/42	to	12/11/43
Wiese, *Hptm* Johannes (acting)	11/5/43	*to*	12/11/43
Wiese, *Hptm* Johannes	13/11/43	to	20/5/44
Borchers, *Hptm* Adolf	11/6/44	to	31/1/45
Hartmann, *Hptm* Erich	1/2/45	to	8/5/45

Key
(+) - Killed, Missing or Failed to Return during service with JG 52

(c.) - circa

II./JG52

von Kornatzki, *Hptm* Hans-Günther	1/9/39	to	26/8/40
Ensslen, *Hptm* Wilhelm	27/8/40	to	2/11/40 (+)
Woitke, *Hptm* Erich	3/11/40	to	28/2/42
Steinhoff, *Hptm* Johannes	1/3/42	to	24/3/43
Kühle, *Hptm* Helmut	25/3/43	to	31/8/43
Barkhorn, *Hptm* Gerhard	1/9/43	to	15/1/45
Lipfert, *Hptm* Helmut (acting)	1/6/44	to	?/10/44
Hartmann, *Hptm* Erich (acting)	16/1/45	to	31/1/45
Batz, *Hptm* Wilhelm	1/2/45	to	8/5/45

III./JG 52

von Houwald, *Hptm* Wolf Heinrich	1/3/40	to	24/7/40 (+)
Ensslen, *Hptm* Wilhelm (acting)	25/7/40	to	31/7/40
von Winterfeld, *Hptm* Alexander	1/8/40	to	6/10/40
Handrick, *Maj* Gotthard	c. 7/10/40	to	22/6/41
Blumensaat, *Maj* Albert	23/6/41	to	23/9/41
Hörnig, *Hptm* Franz (acting)	24/9/41	to	c. 12/41
von Bonin, *Hptm* Hubertus	c. 1/42	to	5/7/43
Rall, *Maj* Günther	6/7/43	to	18/4/44
Haiböck, *Hptm* Josef (acting)	12/43	to	1/44
Hartmann, *Oblt* Erich (acting)	19/4/44	to	28/5/44
Batz, *Hptm* Wilhelm	19/4/44	to	31/1/45
Borchers, *Maj* Adolf	1/2/45	to	8/5/45

APPENDIX 2

AWARD WINNERS

All JG 52 winners of the Knight's Cross, and its higher grades, are presented here chronologically, with their scores at the time of the award(s) noted in brackets

	Knight's Cross	Oak Leaves	Swords	Fate
Leesmann, *Olt* Karl-Heinz	23/7/41 (22)			
Steinhoff, *Olt/Hptm* Johannes	30/8/41 (35)	2/9/42 (101)		
Köppen, *Fw* Gerhard	18/12/41 (40)	27/2/42 (72)		(+)
Graf, *Lt* Hermann (1)	24/1/42 (42)	17/5/42 (93)	19/5/42 (106)	
Steinbatz, *Fw/Ofw* Leopold	14/2/42 (42)	2/6/42 (83)	23/6/42 (99)*	(+)
Rossmann, *Fw* Edmund	19/3/42 (42)			
Dickfeld, *Lt* Adolf	19/3/42 (47)	19/5/42 (101)		
Wachowiak, *Uffz* Friedrich	5/4/42 (46)			
Zwernemann, *Ofw* Josef	23/6/42 (57)	31/10/42 (101)		
Gratz, *Uffz* Karl	1/7/42 (54)			
Grislawski, *Fw* Alfred	1/7/42 (40)			
Simsch, *Olt* Siegfried	1/7/42 (45)			
Steffen, *Fw* Karl	1/7/42 (44)			(+)
Ahnert, *Ofw* Heinz-Wilhelm	23/8/42 (57)*			(+)
Barkhorn , *Olt/Hptm* Gerhard	23//8/42 (59)	11/1/43 (120)	2/3/44 (250)	
Dammers, *Fw* Hans	23/8/42 (51)			(+)
Schmidt, *Lt* Heinz	23/8/42 (51)	16/9/42 (102)		(+)
Rall, *Olt/Hptm* Günther	3/9/42 (65)	26/10/42 (100)	12/9/43 (200)	
Semelka, *Lt* Waldemar	4/9/42 (65)*			(+)
Süss, *Ofw* Ernst	4/9/42 (50)			
Resch, *Hptm* Rudolf	6/9/42 (50)			
Grassmuck, *Ofw* Berthold	19/9/42 (56)			(+)
Hammerl, *Ofw* Karl	19/9/42 (50)			(+)
Bennemann, *Hptm* Helmut	2/10/42 (50)			
Füllgrabe, *Ofw* Heinrich	2/10/42 (52)			(+)
Krupinski, *Lt/Olt* Walter	29/10/42 (53)	2/3/44 (177)		
Miethig, *Lt* Rudolf	29/10/42 (50)			(+)
von Bonin, *Maj* Hubertus	21/12/42 (51)			
Freuwörth, *Ofw* Wilhelm	5/1/43 (56)			
Wiese, *Hptm* Johannes	5/1/43 (51)	2/3/44 (125)		
Nemitz, *Ofw* Willi	11/3/43 (54)			(+)
Denk, *Olt* Gustav	14/3/43 (67)*			(+)
Trenkel, *Ofw* Rudolf	19/8/43 (75)			
Korts, *Lt* Berthold	29/8/43 (113)*			(+)
Hartmann, *Lt/Olt* Erich (2)	29/10/43 (148)	2/3/44 (200)	4/7/44 (239)	
Hrabak, *Obstlt* Dietrich (3)	25/1/43 (118)			
Quast, *Fhj-Ofw* Werner	31/12/43 (84)			
Waldmann, *Lt* Hans	5/2/44 (84)			
Petermann, *Lt* Viktor	29/2/44 (60)			
Obleser, *Lt* Friedrich	23/3/44 (80)			
Batz, *Olt/Hptm* Wilhelm	26/3/44 (75)	20/7/44 (175)	21/4/45 (c.235)	
Fönnekold, *Lt* Otto	26/3/44 (100+)			(+)
Sturm, *Lt* Heinrich	26/3/44 (82)			(+)

	Knight's Cross	Oak Leaves	Swords	Fate
Lipfert, *Lt* Helmut	5/4/44 (90)			
Bunzek, *Lt* Johann	6/4/44 (75)*			(+)
Dähne, *Olt* Paul-Heinrich	6/4/44 (74)			
Düttmann, *Lt* Peter	9/5/44 (91)			
Hoffmann, *Fhj-Fw* Gerhard	14/5/44 (125)			(+)
Sachsenberg, *Fhj-Fw* Heinz	9/6/44 (101)			
Woidich, *Olt* Franz	9/6/44 (80)			
Bachnick, *Lt* Herbert	27/7/44 (79)			(+)
Birkner, *Lt* Hans-Joachim	27/7/44 (98)			(+)
Wolfrum, *Lt* Walter	27/7/44 (126)			
Schall, *Lt* Franz	10/10/44 (117)			
Resch, *Olt* Anton	7/4/45 (c.90)			
Ewald, *Lt* Heinz	20/4/45 (82)			
Haas, *Lt* Freidrich	?/4/45 (74)*			(+)

Key

(1) - plus Diamonds on 16/9/42 (172)

(2) - plus Diamonds on 25/8/44 (301)

(3) - received Knight's Cross while serving with JG 54

(+) - Killed, Missing or Failed to Return during service with JG 52

(*) - awarded posthumously

(c.) - circa

APPENDIX 3

JG 52's CENTURIONS

Hartmann, *Maj* Erich	352	Schall, *Hptm* Franz*	133
Barkhorn, *Maj* Gerhard*	301	Wiese, *Maj* Johannes*	133
Rall, *Maj* Günther*	275	Borchers, *Maj* Adolf	132
Batz, *Maj* Wilhelm	237	Dickfeld, *Maj* Adolf*	132
Graf, *Oberst* Hermann*	212	Ihlefeld, *Oberst* Herbert*	132
Lipfert, *Hptm* Helmut*	203	Hoffmann, *Lt* Gerhard	130
Krupinski, *Maj* Walter*	197	Zwernemann, *Olt* Josef	126
Steinhoff, *Oberst* Johannes*	178	Hrabak, *Oberst* Dietrich*	125
Schmidt, *Hptm* Heinz	173	Obleser, *Lt* Friedrich	120
Sturm, *Hptm* Heinrich	158	Birkner, *Lt* Hans-Joachim	117
Düttmann, *Lt* Peter	152	Dammers, *Lt* Hans	113
Gratz, *Lt* Karl	138	Korts, *Lt* Berthold	113
Trenkel, *Hptm* Rudolf*	138	Woidlich, *Olt* Franz*	110
Wolfrum, *Olt* Walter	137	Sachsenberg, *Lt* Heinz*	104
Fönnekold, *Olt* Otto	136	Miethig, *Hptm* Rudolf	101
Waldmann, *Olt* Hans*	134		
Grislawski, *Hptm* Alfred	133	* Also served with other unit(s)	

COLOUR PLATES

1

Bf 109D-1 'Yellow 1' of Oberleutnant Helmut Kühle, Staffelkapitän 3./JG 433, Böblingen, March 1939

Representative of the machines that first equipped the Geschwader (in its initial guise as JG 433), Kühle's Dora wears standard pre-war finish and markings. As was common with many units at that time, the Staffel colour (yellow) was not just used for the aircraft's individual numeral, but was also added to the spinner tip. Unlike the D-1s, which equipped the Staffel for a scant five months, Hemut Kühle remained its Kapitän for over two years before his transfer to the Geschwaderstab in April 1941. He later became Gruppenkommandeur of II./JG 52 in Russia.

2

Avia B 534 'White 4' of 4./JG 52, Bad Aibling, September 1939

II./JG 52 could boast of more exotic origins. Its 4. Staffel came into being as 1./JG 71, and was briefly equipped with ex-Czech air force Avia B 534 biplanes (in their original overall khaki finish with Luftwaffe markings superimposed). The Staffel operated both open and closed-cockpit versions of the B 534, and some – like 'White 4' depicted here – carried the unit's short-lived 'winged devil' badge on the rear fuselage.

3

Arado Ar 68F 'Red N+11' of 11.(N)/JG 72, Nellingen, September 1939

5./JG 52 also had its beginnings in one of the 'emergency programme' Jagdstaffeln activated in the weeks leading up to the outbreak of war. In this case the unit concerned was 11.(N)/JG 72, which was initially intended for the nightfighter role – hence the 'N' (for Nacht = night) ahead of the fuselage cross. Note too the lengthened exhaust pipes extending below the lower wings to reduce the glare during night flying.

4

Bf 109E (Wk-Nr 3335) 'Red 1' of Leutnant Hans Berthel, 2./JG 52, Bonn-Hangelar, October 1939

Wearing textbook finish and markings of the period, this is the early Emil in which Hans Berthel claimed I. Gruppe's first kill of the war – a French LeO 451 16 miles (26 km) southwest of Bonn on 6 October 1939. At this early stage of the hostilities the number '1' machine was customarily the mount of the Staffelkapitän. But if Wk-Nr 3335 was, in fact, the usual machine of future Knight's Cross winner Oberleutnant Wolfgang Ewald, there is no record as to why Leutnant Berthel happened to be flying it on this occasion.

5

Bf 109E 'Red 1' of Oberleutnant August-Wilhelm Schumann, Staffelkapitän 5./JG 52, Mannheim, November 1939

In accordance with contemporary regulations, this 'Red 1' (of II. Gruppe) was flown by 5./JG 52's Staffelkapitän. The unit's nightfighter Arados had not lasted long – and neither would the experimental, disruptive three-tone camouflage pattern seen here being sported by 'Shorty' Schumann's machine. By January 1940 his Emil was already resplendent in a new coat of hellblau paint. Unlike I. and III. Gruppen, II./JG 52 never introduced a common Gruppe badge. Instead, each Staffel opted for its own device, 5./JG 52's being a little red devil wielding a bow and arrow.

6

Bf 109E 'Yellow 1' of Oberleutnant Werner Lederer, Staffelkapitän 6./JG 52, Luxemborg-Sandweiler, June 1940

Depicted towards the end of the French campaign, Lederer's machine displays a typical early 1940 hellblau respray finish (with high demarcation line along the dorsal spine). Other points of interest are the Staffel's elaborate eagle motif on the cowling (which was either painted in solid black, as here, or applied in a more simplified stencil form), the name Hans Eck below the cockpit (carried by several of Lederer's aircraft in honour of a fallen comrade), the diagonal red line from wingroot step to cockpit sill and, finally, the two kill bars on the rudder for a Potez 63 and Bloch 210, claimed on 4 and 6 June respectively.

7

Bf 109E 'Yellow 12' of 9./JG 52, Hoppstädten, June 1940

Also shown at the time of the Blitzkrieg, this Emil serves to illustrate two of the unusual marking practices which made III./JG 52's machines stand out from all others of that period – the application of a distinctive dark green 'cross-hatching' pattern to tone down the hellblau fuselage sides, and the use of overly large and broad individual aircraft numerals and a Gruppe wavy bar symbol. The former would not long survive the Battle of Britain era, but the latter were still in evidence at the start of Barbarossa.

8

Bf 109E 'Black Chevron and Bars' of Major Hanns Trübenbach, Geschwaderkommodore JG 52, Calais-Marck, September 1940

The Kommodore's machine wears a more common light dapple finish over its basic hellblau scheme, plus standard command markings and Battle of Britain yellow cowling and rudder. No sign yet, though, of the Geschwader emblem Hanns Trübenbach was about to introduce in order to instil a sense of collective identity in his three hitherto disparate Gruppen. The design he selected was a shield in red and black – the colours of Württemberg, the Stab's home province – bisected by a silver winged sword.

9

Bf 109E 'Black Double Chevron' of Hauptmann Wolfgang Ewald, Gruppenkommandeur I./JG 52, Katwijk, January 1941

Bearing more than a superficial resemblance to the Kommodore's Emil above, Ewald's machine is wearing the new Geschwader badge in what was to become its customary place below the windscreen (on both sides of the fuselage). Note that this has displaced I. Gruppe's own 'running boar' emblem, which had adorned the cowlings of the unit's fighters since the autumn of 1939. This latter was now much reduced in size, and relegated to the rear fuselage aft of the Balkenkreuz.

10

Bf 109E 'Black 10' of 5./JG 52, Raversidje, April 1941

Guarding the North Sea coast in the spring of 1941 – although still wearing the undappled *hellblau* finish more usually associated with the spring of 1940 (albeit with Channel front yellow tactical markings added) – this machine of 5./JG 52 demonstrates that *Staffel* badges were also greatly reduced in size (compare with profile 5) in order not to detract from the new *Geschwader* emblem. Note, too, that 5. *Staffel's* individual numerals have already changed from the earlier (regulation) red to black – *before* the unit's transfer to the eastern front, where the colour red was almost universally avoided to prevent confusion with Soviet air force markings.

11

Bf 109E 'Black 4' of Gefreiter Friedrich Wachowiak, 8./JG 52, Bucharest-Pipera, April 1941

Despite its temporary redesignation as I./JG 28 when despatched to Rumania in late 1940, III./JG 52 made no attempt to disguise or delete its tell-tale large wavy bar III. *Gruppe* symbols. However, when subsequently involved in the Balkans campaign, the application of yellow theatre markings *did* obscure the unit's 'wolf' badge on the cowlings of its machines. Note that, in addition to yellow cowling and rudder, this *Emil* also carries narrow yellow bands aft of the fuselage cross and just inboard of the wingtips. The unusual style of the '4' is noteworthy too.

12

Bf 109F 'Black Chevron 4' of the *Gruppenstab* I./JG 52, Katwijk, September 1941

Remaining part of the North Sea coastal defence force long after the launch of *Barbarossa*, I./JG 52 applied a camouflage of its own devising to several of its recently delivered *Friedrichs*. The three-tone finish depicted here was considered more suitable for overwater operations. In addition, this machine sports the new *Gruppe* badge. Replacing the 'running boar', it too was more in keeping with the unit's current role, and depicting a black hand grasping an RAF machine (Spitfire?) above the North Sea. Lastly, note the individual numeral behind the *Stab* chevron. This combination, which indicated both the pilot's office (in this instance, adjutant) and his position in the *Stabsschwarm* (No 4), was to be found quite frequently on machines of JG 52.

13

Bf 109F 'Black Chevrons and Bars' of Major Hanns Trübenbach, *Geschwaderkommodore* JG 52, Tiraspol, October 1941

Major Trübenbach's *Friedrich* wears the dark green finish more usually associated with JG 77 (see *Osprey Aircraft of the Aces 37 - Bf 109 Aces of the Russian Front* profiles 39 and 40 for aircraft from this unit). The somewhat unusual position of the yellow band ahead of the *Balkenkreuz*, rather than around the rear fuselage, is also reminiscent of the same unit (then based in the Ukraine) – all of which might seem to suggest that this is an ex-JG 77 machine (note also the overpainted individual numeral of a previous owner). But would a *Kommodore* be flying a hand-me-down aircraft? Whatever the true facts, the full set of command markings, plus the *Geschwader* badge

Trübenbach himself introduced, are proof positive of present ownership.

14

Bf 109F 'Black 7' of 2./JG 52, Rusa, November 1941

On the subject of badges, this Bf 109F of 2. *Staffel* – in otherwise standard finish for the autumn of 1941 – is indicative of a period of transition. It displays I. *Gruppe's* new 'black hand' emblem on the engine cowling, as well as the unit's earlier 'running boar' crest on the rear fuselage. At this same time the *Friedrichs* of 3./JG 52 were also sporting two badges – the 'black hand' on the cowling and their own *Staffel* shield aft of the *Balkenkreuz*. The latter, adopted towards the close of the unit's North Sea service, depicted a stream of bullets slicing Chamberlain's umbrella in two. Already anachronistic (Chamberlain had long been replaced by Churchill), this device was even more out of place in the Ukraine, and was soon discarded altogether.

15

Bf 109F 'Black 12' of 5./JG 52, Byelgorod, June 1942

Meanwhile, 5. *Staffel's* 'little devil' soldiered on regardless. Here it is seen – admittedly still in its much reduced state – adorning the cowling of a densely dappled machine in the summer of 1942. Note the much more prominent *Geschwader* badge, and the very wide aft fuselage yellow band occupying all of the space between the *Balkenkreuz* and the tail unit.

16

Bf 109G-2 'Black Double Chevron' of Hauptmann Johannes Steinhoff, *Gruppenkommandeur* II./JG 52, Rostov, August, 1942

It was only when the unit converted from *Friedrichs* to new Bf 109Gs in the late summer of 1942 that II./JG 52 finally began to conform to regulations by applying a standard II. *Gruppe* horizontal bar to the rear fuselage of its machines. For nearly three years the unit had, for some unknown reason, steadfastly refused to adopt the accepted II. *Gruppe* symbol. Note that *Kommandeur* Steinhoff's *Gustav* also has the closely dappled cowling panels which featured on a number of II./JG 52 fighters during this period.

17

Bf 109G-2 'Yellow 5' of Leutnant Walter Krupinski, 6./JG 52, Armavir, August 1942

Leutnant Krupinski's G-2 also dutifully wears a standard II. *Gruppe* horizontal bar symbol – and in the correct *Staffel* colour of yellow to boot! Note too that, unlike the machine above, it is sporting the *Geschwader's* 'winged sword' badge – an item that was slated soon to disappear in the security clamp-down intended to 'deny intelligence to the enemy'.

18

Bf 109G-2 'Black 13' of Oberleutnant Günther Rall, *Staffelkapitän* 8./JG 52, Gostanovka, August 1942

Another victim of the security drive to abolish distinctive unit badges, and thus disguise aircraft movements (which in turn revealed to the Soviets just how thinly-stretched the Luftwaffe was becoming!), would be III. *Gruppe's* recently introduced 'barbed cross' emblem, as displayed here on 8. *Staffel's* 'Black 13'. Although this particular machine has long been associated with the world's third-ranking fighter pilot, Günther Rall flew it only occasionally. His usual mount at this time, in accordance with his position as *Staffelkapitän*, was 'Black 1'.

19

Bf 109G-2 'Yellow 11' of Oberleutnant Hermann Graf, *Staffelkapitän* 9./JG 52, Pitomnik, September 1942
Rall's fellow *Kapitän*, Oberleutnant Hermann Graf of the famed *'Karaya' Staffel* (note the emblem below the cockpit), flew a *Gustav* very similar to that depicted above, albeit with the individual aircraft number and III. *Gruppe* wavy bar in 9. *Staffel's* obligatory yellow. This is reportedly the machine that Graf was piloting when he claimed his 150th victory on 4 September (as leader of the Stalingrad *Kommando* operating out of Tazinskaya). But it was his 'Yellow 1' – again the *Staffelkapitän's* customary mount – which carried Graf's scoreboard on its rudder.

20

Bf 109G-2/R6 'White 3' of 1./JG 52, Rostov, November 1942
I./JG 52 had received its first 'gunboats' (in the form of F-4/R1s) in spring 1942. This later *Gustav*, similarly armed with two additional MG 151 cannon in underwing gondolas, was one of a number taken on charge later the same year. The additional firepower of these machines was used to great effect, both in the air against the heavily-armoured *Sturmoviks*, as well as against a variety of ground targets, including locomotives, tanks, soft-skinned vehicles and artillery emplacements.

21

Bf 109G-4 'Yellow 3' of Unteroffizier Hans Waldmann, 6./JG 52, Anapa, June 1943
Flown by Hans 'Dackel' Waldmann – one of the best of the younger *'Nachwuchs'*, or second-generation, pilots to make their mark in the latter half of the war – this newly delivered G-4 still displays evidence of an (overpainted) factory four-letter code on its fuselage flanks. There is no longer any sign of a unit badge, but note the personal emblem below the cockpit. A word-play on the pilot's nickname, Waldmann (woodsman) is also a favourite name for a pet dachshund – colloquially a *Dackel* – in Germany.

22

Bf 109G-4 'Black 12' of Leutnant Peter Düttmann, 5./JG 52, Anapa, July 1943
Wearing neither unit nor personal badges, this anonymous 5. *Staffel Gustav* serves to illustrate the smaller style numerals (see also profile above) that II. *Gruppe* was favouring in mid-1943. It was in this 'Black 12' that future Knight's Cross winner Peter 'Bonifaz' Düttmann claimed 5./JG 52's 500th victory over the Kuban bridgehead on 15 July .

23

Bf 109G-6 'Black Double Chevron' of Hauptmann Johannes Wiese, acting-*Gruppenkommandeur* I./JG 52, Varvarovka, July 1943
While serving as the acting *Kommandeur* of I. *Gruppe* (from 11 May to 12 November 1943), Johannes Wiese

usually flew this G-6 *Beule*, adorned with the appropriate command chevrons. It was his chosen mount for the opening day of *Zitadelle*, when he was credited with 12 victories (numbers 84 to 95). And Wiese was flying it again five days later when he became a centurion.

24

Bf 109G-6 'Black Double Chevron' of Hauptmann Gerhard Barkhorn, *Gruppenkommandeur* II./JG 52, Poltava-North, September 1943
Already wearing the Oak Leaves, and rapidly approaching his double century, Gerhard Barkhorn also flew a *Gustav* sporting double chevrons as befitted his recent appointment as *Kommandeur* of II. *Gruppe*. But note the two additions which helped to personalise this otherwise standard G-6 – his wife's name *Christl* below the cockpit sill, and the small 5 – Barkhorn's lucky number – applied between the arms of the command chevron. Sadly, luck ran out for both Gerhard and Christl Barkhorn in January 1983 when they were killed in an accident on the Cologne Autobahn.

25

Bf 109G-6 'Black Chevron and Bars' of Oberstleutnant Dietrich Hrabak, *Geschwaderkommodore* JG 52, Kerch V, October 1943
JG 52's sixth, and longest serving *Kommodore*, Dietrich Hrabak flew this G-6 approximately halfway through his tenure of office when the *Geschwaderstab* was based on the complex of airfields around Kerch on the eastern tip of the Crimean Peninsula, together with I. *Gruppe* (at Kerch IV) and elements of II./JG 52. The textbook command insignia clearly indicate this to be the machine of a *Kommodore*, but offer no clue to enemy intelligence as to the unit's actual identity.

26

Bf 109G-6 'Yellow 1' of Leutnant Erich Hartmann, *Staffelkapitän* 9./JG 52, Novo-Zaporozhe, October 1943
By this time, however, the *'Karaya' Staffel* had become so well known on the eastern front that it positively flaunted its identity, not merely retaining its now familiar 'pierced heart' emblem (see profile 19) in defiance of standing instructions, but sometimes even adding its equally famous callsign below. Despite the 121 victories recorded on the rudder, 'Yellow 1's' pilot was not yet a household name – he was then still 27 kills short of his Knight's Cross! It would be some months before Erich Hartmann began proclaiming his presence in the air to both friend and foe alike by adding the distinctive black 'tulip leaf' to the nose of every aircraft he flew.

27

Bf 109G-6 'Black 15' of Leutnant Walter Wolfrum, 5./JG 52, Gramatikovo, March 1944
Shorn of unit badges, many fighters were given individual names instead. Walter Wolfrum chose to christen his machine *Quex*, possibly after the accident-prone pilot who was the hero of a popular film series of the time. But perhaps Wolfrum was tempting fate. This particular 'Black 15' (Wk-Nr 411 777) was destroyed in a crash-landing after tangling with *Sturmoviks* over the Crimea in April 1944. And in July Wolfrum himself was so severely wounded that he was off operations for six months.

28

Bf 109G-6 'Yellow 3' of Leutnant Heinz Ewald, 6./JG 52, Zilistea, June 1944

Another of the *Geschwader's* highly successful second-generation Knight's Cross winners (see profiles 21, 22 and 27), 'Esau' Ewald flew this G-6 'gunboat' during II. *Gruppe's* brief deployment to Rumania to protect the Ploesti oilfields against attack by US heavy bombers based in Italy. 'Yellow 3' also sported a personal emblem – in this case a wordplay on the pilot's nickname 'E-sow'.

29

Bf 109G-6 'White 1' of Hauptmann Erich Hartmann, *Staffelkapitän* 4./JG 52, Budaörs, November 1944

Unarguably the most famous 'second-generationer' of them all – not just within the ranks of JG 52, but of the entire *Jagdwaffe* – was Erich Hartmann. Although by this time *Kapitän* of the newly-reformed 4./JG 52, Hartmann has elected to keep the *'Karaya'* heart as his personal emblem (albeit without the arrow), with his fiancée's name superimposed on it. But it is that striking nose decoration which advertises the now triple-centurion's presence to all and sundry, and which – if the wartime press is to be believed – earned him the nickname of the 'Black Devil of the South' from his opponents.

30

Bf 109G-10 'Yellow 4' of 6./JG 52, Veszprem, February 1945

In stark contrast to the defiant flamboyance of Hartmann's *Gustav* immediately above, most of the *Geschwader's* machines wore a cloak of absolute anonymity as the war entered its final weeks. With no clue as to its actual unit identity, the only information to be gleaned from this G-10 is that it belonged to an unknown 6. *Staffel* (yellow individual numeral and horizontal II. *Gruppe* bar), and that it was operating on the Hungarian sector of the front (yellow chevron below the port wing).

31

Bf 109G-14 'White 8' of 4./JG 52, Fels-am-Wagram, April 1945

Representative of II. *Gruppe's* final equipment – a mix of G-10s and G-14s – this late *Gustav* still displays the broad yellow nose band which displaced the underwing chevron (see above) as the tactical recognition marking of all fighters operating over Hungary (II./JG 52 had retired from Vat, in Hungary, to Vienna-Götzendorf on 28 March). Subsequently departing Austria for surrender to US forces in southern Germany, the personnel of II./JG 52 were the only members of the *Geschwader* to escape post-war Soviet captivity.

32

Bf 109G-14 'Yellow 10' of 3./JG 52, Deutsch Brod (Nemecky Brod), May 1945

Reconstructed from wreckage abandoned at Deutsch Brod as members of I. and III. *Gruppe* set off for the German border by road, this profile (and its reference sources) illustrate not only the completely anonymous finish worn – but also the ultimate fate suffered – at war's end by most of the machines of what had once been, and still remains to this day, the most successful fighter unit in the history of aerial warfare.

BIBLIOGRAPHY

BRACKE, GERHARD, *Gegen vielfache Übermacht.* Motorbuch-Verlag, Stuttgart, 1977

CARELL, PAUL, *Unternehmen Barbarossa.* Ullstein, Frankfurt/M, 1963

CONSTABLE, TREVOR J and TOLIVER, COL RAYMOND F (ret), *Horrido! Fighter Aces of the Luftwaffe.* Macmillan, New York, 1968

EWALD, HEINZ, *Esau.* (Eigenverlag), Coburg, 1990

FAST, NIKO, *Das Jagdgeschwader 52* (2 vols.). Bensberger Buch-Verlag, Bergisch Gladbach, 1990

GÜTH, FRANK/PAUL, AXEL/SCHUH, HORST, *Vom Feindflug nicht zurückgekehrt.* Helios, Aachen, 2001

HELD, WERNER, *Die deutschen Jagdgeschwader im Russlandfeldzug.* Podzun-Pallas-Verlag, Friedberg, 1986

KUROWSKI, FRANZ, *Balkenkreuz und Roter Stern.* Podzun-Pallas-Verlag, Friedberg, 1984

LIPFERT, HELMUT, *Das Tagebuch des Hauptmann Lipfert.* Motorbuch-Verlag, Stuttgart, 1973

MEHNERT, KURT und TEUBER, REINHARD, *Die deutsche Luftwaffe 1939-1945.* Militär-Verlag Patzwall, Norderstedt, 1996

NOWARRA, HEINZ J, *Luftwaffen-Einsatz "Barbarossa" 1941.* Podzun-Pallas-Verlag, Friedberg

OBERMAIER, ERNST, *Die Ritterkreuzträger der Luftwaffe 1939-1945: Band 1, Jagdflieger.* Verlag Dieter Hoffmann, Mainz, 1966

PLOCHER, Generalleutnant HERMANN, *The German Air Force versus Russia, 1942/1943* (2 vols). Arno Press, New York, 1966/67

PRIEN, JOCHEN, et al,, *Die Jagdfliegerverbände der Deutschen Luftwaffe 1943 bis 1945* (various vols.), struve-druck, Eutin, 2000

SCHREIER, HANS, *JG 52.* Kurt Vowinckel-Verlag, Berg am See, 1990

TOLIVER, COL RAYMOND F (ret) and CONSTABLE, TREVOR J, *The Blond Knight of Germany,* Doubleday & Co, New York, 1970

INDEX

References to illustrations are shown in **bold**. Plates are shown with page and caption locators in (brackets).